Confessions of a Nerdy Girl:

Diary #5

TRUTH OR DARE

by Linda Rey
www.NerdyGirlBooks.com

Confessions of a Nerdy Girl: Diary #5

Truth or Dare: Confessions of a Nerdy Girl Diary Series, Book #5 is a work of fiction. Names, characters, places, and incidents either are the product of the author's imagination or are used fictitiously. Any resemblance to actual persons, living or dead, events, or locales is entirely coincidental.

Copyright © 2022 Pretty Bird Literary

ISBN: 978-1-949557-10-7

All rights reserved

Cover art by www.fiverr.com/Nizar86

Summary: A self-professed nerdy girl struggles with the breakup of her family, the death of her pet, and the challenges of middle school, in diary entries dedicated to "M"—the mother who left her at an orphanage twelve years ago.

Nerdy Girl books by Linda Rey

Diary Series:

TOP SECRET: Diary #1 (Confessions of a Nerdy Girl Diaries)

UNLUCKY THIRTEEN: Diary #2 (Confessions of a Nerdy Girl Diaries)

LETTERS FROM SUMMER CAMP: Diary #3 (Confessions of a Nerdy Girl Diaries)

LETTERS TO SANTA, THE EASTER BUNNY, AND OTHER LAME STUFF: Diary #4 (Confessions of a Nerdy Girl Diaries)

TRUTH OR DARE: Diary #5 (Confessions of a Nerdy Girl Diaries)

SUNNY SIDE OVER: Diary #6 (Confessions of a Nerdy Girl Diaries) Coming Soon!

Novel Series:

NERDY EVER AFTER: A Nerdy Novel, Book 1 (Confessions of a Nerdy Girl)

CHECK OUT ALL OF THE NEWEST TITLES AND OTHER NERDY NEWS AT:

www.nerdygirlbooks.com

For Jessica,

who makes the world a better place.

Confessions of a Nerdy Girl: Diary #5

Table of Contents

MOURNFUL MONDAY, 8:29 P.M. 1

TRAUMATIC TUESDAY, 7:59 P.M. 8

WACKY WEDNESDAY, 7:15 P.M. 21

WACKY WEDNESDAY, PART 2, 7:25 P.M. 30

ANOTHER ZOMBIE SLOG DAY,
9:02 P.M. 34

A BRA STORY, 10:51 P.M. 41

WILLA RAMBLINGS, 10:13 A.M. 57

SOME DOOZIE NEWSIE, 6:24 P.M. 68

SUNLESS SUNDAY, 8:08 P.M. 76

WHINY WEDNESDAY CONT., 4:27 P.M. ...90

IN MEMORIUM: RIP REGGIE, 9:21 P.M. ...99

JUST ANOTHER MONDAY, 6:59 P.M. .. 109

TRUTH OR DARE, 5:15 P.M. 114

TRUTH OR DARE, CONT., 5:21 P.M. 117

ANOTHER UGLY PUGLY DAY,
7:47 P.M. 131

A RAINY FRIDAY, 8:02 P.M. 136

GRATITUDE SUNDAY, 10:10 A.M. 148
NERDY GIRL BOOKS BY LINDA REY 154
ABOUT THE AUTHOR 155

MOURNFUL MONDAY, 8:29 P.M.

Dear M,

Today I ran away from home.

It was a horrible experience, and I don't recommend it.

(Although, in full disclosure, NO actual "running" took place. It would be more accurate to say that I ambled away or I meandered. I moseyed, or I strolled. Besides, I only made it around the block before my dad found me.)

The reasons I don't recommend running away are because: (A) It's "fraught" with danger (fraught is my word for the day. It means filled with something.) and (B) Because it makes the ones you leave behind super sad. (There are a bunch of other reasons too, but those are my top.)

My dad was so sad that when he found me, he masked it with anger. It sounds confusing to explain it this way, but if you knew my dad, you'd know that usually, he's super nice and easy-going, but that when he's sad or afraid, his face gets red and splotchy and his lips scrunch together like he's sucked on a lemon. So he looks mad in the middle of his face, but then his eyes turn down at the outside corners and droop like a cartoon hound dog. (If you've ever seen a cartoon hound dog, you'd know they all seem a bit melancholy.)

When my dad found me, he slowed the Prius to a crawl, and he yelled through the open window, "WILLA EUGENIA SHISBEY, GET IN THIS CAR — NOW!!"

I had no choice but to open the door and climb inside. And not just because my dad was hollering at me in the middle of the street, but because I had a terrible stitch in my side, and I knew I didn't have the physical stamina to make it any farther than my middle school, a few blocks away.

When I got in the car, my dad demanded "some answers."

ANSWERS!!

He lost his angry-dad steam as soon as I sat down, and his voice seemed shaky. And I saw tears sparkling in his eyes even through his black-framed glasses.

"Please don't ever scare me like that! Promise me, Willa, that you will never do that to me again," he said. And then he asked me why I ran away.

I explained how it wasn't fair that, because of me, he and Diane were getting a divorce and how he was losing his REAL daughter too. (Although, M, if you knew Diane and Olivia, you'd see why some people might think it wasn't the worst thing that could happen to a person.)

I told my dad that if I was no longer in the picture, maybe Diane would come home, and then they could all be a family again.

Hope

By that time, my eyes were so blurry from MY tears that I could hardly see, and there was a huge weight on my chest that pressed me back against the car's seat and made it hard to breathe.

My dad said (and by then, he was sort of crying too, or maybe he just had something stuck in his eye because he took off his glasses and wiped the corners with the hem of his shirt), "Willa, I will NEVER be better off without you. NEVER!!" And the second never was even more forceful than the first, so I knew he totally meant it. Then my dad said that I was "the daughter of his choosing" and that adopting me was one of the BEST decisions of his life.

Ü ♡✫ ⚘

"Daughter of his choosing," he'd said, and it made me cry harder because who doesn't want to be "Chosen?" (Just ask any kid when it's time to make a selection to be on a sports team or a girl who wants to be asked to the prom by the boy she likes.)

"Scout's honor?" I asked my dad, my heart swelling with love and gratitude for his choice to keep me when Diane gave him the ultimatum that it was her or me.

My dad smiled at my lame choice of words, considering I've never been a Scout myself.

"Scout's honor," he said.

And then he raised two fingers to his right eye in what I guessed to be a Scout Salute.

It was a bit of a weep fest after that. Not so much on my Dad's part, who held it together, but on my part.

Mostly I cried out of happiness. Happiness that my dad is willing to fight for me, whatever the cost. And I cried in appreciation that my dad had come to look for me because honestly, M, I don't know where I would have gone. I think a part of me thought … and don't get freaked out … (because it was a small, itsy-bitsy teeny-tiny part) that maybe I'd try to find

YOU by going to the last place I saw you, The Children's Home Society of Chicago, and begging for information.

But then sanity returned, and it gave me a noogie to the head before saying, "HELLOOOO!!! Earth to Willa!" and I realized that if you wanted to see me, the child you abandoned, that you would have found a way by now.

love

Willa

Confessions of a Nerdy Girl: Diary #5

TRAUMATIC TUESDAY, 7:59 P.M.

Dear M,

The divorce drama continues. Ugh!

You can't believe the amount of calls and texts between my dad and Diane. (And yet everyone thinks that teens are the ones who reign supreme when it comes to DRAMA.)

Drama Rama

Like, last night ... when my dad said he wished we had an old-fashioned phone. And he didn't mean a first-generation cell phone with a flip top. He meant the "olden-days" kind of phones you see in black and white movies. The phones that had the hand-held thingy that sat on a cradle, and with the spiral cord that attached the whatchamacallit to the plastic whozeewhatzit. (That case or whatever with the round numbered dial in the middle of it that sounds like a zipper zipping when the dial rotated back to the zero position.)

And I'm like, "Seriously, Dad? WHAT?! WHY?! And HOW?! Just THINKING about being TETHERED to the wall by my phone gives me anxiety," I told him.

Dad explained that if he had the old kind of phone, he could SLAM the hand-held part down on the cradle and hang up on Diane! He says it's much more DRAMATIC than just pressing a button and silently ending a call because it's super loud on the other end, and the person knows you hung up on purpose and you didn't just lose them because your phone service isn't 5G or whatever.

Can you hear me now??

I gave my dad a major eye roll and told him he needed a time-out and to go to his room to contemplate his poor behavior. Ha!

The OFFICIAL and legal reason for the divorce is something called "Irreconcilable Differences," but that's only because the reason "It's All Willa's Fault" isn't legally recognized in the state of California. (There are currently 16 other "No Fault" states in the U.S.)

I don't mean to imply that it's my fault because I DID something SPECIFIC to end my dad's marriage. (Well, maybe I did, just by being me — a weirdo.) But the reality is that Diane, the person who was my MOM after you, just didn't like me.

I know it sounds as if I'm some whiny nerd complaining that the kids won't play with her, like, "Teacher!" whah whah… "The kids won't play with me!" whah whah. "Nobody likes me." Whah whah…

But the gosh honest truth on why Dad and Diane are divorcing is because Diane, my legal "mother," literally doesn't like me.

I mean. What's not to like, right? (HA!)

According to Diane, I'm odd and quirky (which means "out of the ordinary"), and I don't "blink enough," if you can believe that. She also told my dad that I give her the "creeps" with my big brown eyes, magnified and unblinking, behind my oversized black glasses.

What a laugh!

So let me address some of Diane's other "issues" with me, and you be the judge.

First of all, I'm not odd in some pulls-the-wings-off-of-butterflies scary way. I'm just your regular run-of-the-mill OCD kid who likes clean hands and a tidy sleeping environment. And so sure, maybe my hand washing causes my cuticles to bleed from time to time, and I like to count the cracks in the sidewalk out of sheer boredom on my way to school, but, COME ON, there are probably millions of "normal" kids who do the same. (Or if not millions, then hundreds, at least.)

OK, so I have to admit that Diane is right. I AM quirky. Of all the QUIRKIES in the world, I might be the quirkiest. But my dad says that it's the quality he loves most about me — my quirkiness. That quirky is what makes me "unique." Who wants normal, my dad says. Normal is dull. Normal is boring. Normal is a single scoop of vanilla ice cream in a soggy paper cup.

Quirky, on the other hand, Dad says, well, quirky is a three-scooper on a deluxe waffle cone with multicolored sprinkles. And not just three scoops of a single flavor, but all of the crazy flavored ones, like chocolaty Rocky Road with its squishy marshmallows and chewy nuts, topped with a scoop of velvety Banana Nut Fudge, and then finished with a big round scoop of Butterscotch Ribbon and its gooey goodness, and topped with a handful of rainbow colored sprinkles that rain down the colossal confection for some extra crunch.

And is it wrong to like to COLLECT things? (OK, that toenail clipping collection was pretty gross, but it was also very short-lived, and I was a LITTLE KID at the time, who, until I came to live with the Shisbeys, slept three to a bed in that overcrowded orphanage. If you've ever been forced to sleep on a stinky, wet-with-pee mattress with other toddlers for years on end, it goes without saying that there's bound to be some socially unacceptable behavior for a while after.)

Who doesn't like to collect calendars? Or novelty erasers? Or gum wrappers? (Which has waned in popularity in the last forty or so years but was a popular pastime in my dad's day, or so he says.)

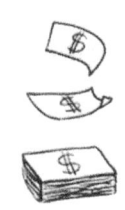

Washing money?

Doesn't EVERYONE? And if they don't, they should. Do people NOT KNOW how dirty money can be? According to the experts, paper money carries more germs and fecal matter (I'm sure you know that "fecal matter" is doctor-speak for POOP) than your average household toilet! Paper bills are hosts for gross microbes: viruses, and bacteria and can survive for 48 hours! Even worse, a live flu virus can survive on a five-spot (or a dollar bill, or a ten...) for up to 17 days! Seventeen days! That's the equivalent of 16 GENERATIONS of mayflies!! (Or half the lifespan of a common housefly, which can live for 28 days.)

Paper money spreads E. Coli ... Salmonella ... Staphylococcus ... MRSA ...

Is it any wonder that I lie awake at night every Friday after my dad has handed me my allowance?

As far as the blinking — or lack of it — I blink plenty. Nine hundred and sixty times an hour, to be exact. (I counted.) An amount still on the "normal" realm, although lower than the twelve hundred times per hour — the high end — for "frequent blinkers."

I won't go into all the details about the divorce, at least not now, but basically, Diane gave my dad an ULTIMATUM, which means a "final demand," the day after she called the orphanage to see if they would take me back.

Yes, you read that correctly!

Diane actually called the orphanage to see if, 9 YEARS LATER!!, she could return me.

Return to Sender!

I heard it from Olivia, who seemed happy to share all the details, that Diane demanded to speak with "The Warden." Which is a laugh and probably a lie because it's an ORPHANAGE, not a prison, and despite what you see in all the movies, some of the staff were pretty nice to us.

Olivia said they told her mom to "take a hike," that adoption doesn't work that way, that there are no "give-backs" when it comes to the orphans, and so Diane was "stuck with me."

As you can imagine, Diane was NOT happy to hear that, and neither was Olivia, who didn't like having a sibling because that meant she had to share a bathroom in addition to all the other sharing of stuff, and Olivia doesn't do "Share."

Just in case you think I'm exaggerating about how mean Olivia is, she once suggested that her mom tie a sign around my neck with the words "FREE" printed in big black letters, add a cute bow to my hair, and plant me in front of PetSmart next to the boxes of kittens and puppies on the next pet adoption day, hoping that someone would, in her words "Take the bait."

Pick me! Pick me!

I don't know if it's OK to reveal TOO much of my dad's personal stuff and be a big tattletale about the divorce (although TECHNICALLY, that's the whole point of a diary — Amirite? To share MY secrets and everyone else's?) but let me tell you about the last family dinner. A dinner when the tension in our house was so thick that it sucked the air from the room and made it impossible for us to eat (plus the meatloaf was gross and dry, so there's that).

Diane looked over at my dad, and she said, "Ted, I need to talk with you. Pass the salt." My dad passed the salt, then he put down his fork and took off his glasses, and cleaned them with his napkin.

"I'm right here, Diane," Dad said, stating the obvious.

"ALONE!" Diane snapped, and Olivia rolled her eyes like she does every time her mom gets overly dramatic.

We all knew dinner was over after that, and my dad and Diane walked towards their bedroom on the other side of the house with me following a safe distance behind, where I stood and listened in once they closed and locked the door.

And if I live to be a hundred (which is becoming more likely, what with technology and all), I'll never forget the words coming from behind the closed door from the woman who was supposed to be my mother...

"It's your choice, Ted," I heard Diane say, her voice loud and shrill. "You can have Willa, or you can have me. But you cannot have both!"

I held my breath, M. And I prayed.

I prayed really, really hard as fat sloppy tears drooled down my face, hoping that my prayers would be heard and even making ridiculous promises that I knew I couldn't possibly keep (Give up candy forever? Seriously?? Not likely!) if only God would answer my prayers.

And it probably was only seconds, although it seemed like an eternity before my dad responded and my prayers were answered.

"Then I choose Willa," I heard my dad say in a voice that sounded wobbly. "I'm sorry, Diane, but if I have to make a choice, then I choose Willa."

And for that, I will be FOREVER grateful.

Yours in happiness AND sorrow,

Willa

WACKY WEDNESDAY, 7:15 P.M.

Dear M,

Do you remember your dreams?

I do, and I wish I could say that mine are the stuff of Saturday morning cartoons and Pixar flicks: fluffy and colorful and accompanied with a music soundtrack so sickeningly sweet that it gives you a toothache just to listen.

But that's not the case.

My dreams are more like the stuff that horror movies are made of. Not the super gory kind, thank goodness. (I may be "a troubled kid," according to Diane, but I'm not a psycho.) Instead, mine are more like real-life scenarios, like getting trapped in an elevator or falling off a cliff, or barfing in front of my entire class at school.

Which I did once, in fifth grade, I'm embarrassed to say, after having some alphabet SpaghettiOs for lunch. Half the class was so grossed out they almost hurled too, but the other half made a Reading and Writing lesson out of it, shouting out things like "Hey! There's an A!" and "I see an F!" Except for Louis Booker who sat in the seat behind me. Louis said, "Look! How rad! Willa spelled TWO!" (But I'm pretty sure the second letter was an upside-down "M" and not a "W," so I didn't regurgitate a full word, just an undigested "t," an "m," and an "o.")

T... M... O...

And probably, like everyone on the planet, I've had the "Naked in Class" dream, which puts the vomit experience in perspective.

Sure, it was horrifying to barf in class, but even back then I thought ... "Well at least I'm wearing clothes!"

But my first experience with vivid nightmares started the year I turned three, and they were chronic! And I know what you're thinking, "What three-year-old remembers their dreams?" But as I've told you before, I'm "Unlucky Thirteen." I'm the thirteenth person in the world to be documented with something called H-SAM: Highly Superior Autobiographical Memory, which means I can recall with computer accuracy every moment of my pitiful existence since the day you left me at the orphanage, less than twenty-four hours after my first birthday.

H-SAM is a superpower of mine that is essentially useless, except for those rare occasions when I want to remember what I wore to school on the last 37 Tuesdays. (Ha! There's a little more to H-SAM than that, plus the outfits I wear are as boring as I am and not worth remembering.)

It wasn't as though I had a string of DIFFERENT nightmares when I had them. Oh no. It was the SAME reoccurring BATHTUB dream (Yes, "bathtub." I'm a weirdo, I know) week after week, and with the same gruesome ending.

The nightmare wasn't about having to TAKE a bath or anything like that because even at three, I was pretty much an OCD clean freak. I liked smelling fresh and not like a wet puppy, which is what most of my fellow orphans smelled like. I knew that "Water is Our Friend," as the night duty bath-time helper used to remind us.

Instead, my nightmares were brought on because, in real life, I had a major issue with the bathtub DRAIN, as lame as that sounds. I mean, like, I got majorly freaked EVERY TIME the rubber plug was pulled. (Our tubs had these crusty old-fashioned rubber plugs, not the metal push kind).

I'd watch the water with mounting terror as it disappeared with loud gurgles and noisy slurps, the swirling vortex of water, a mini tornado, sucking everything in its path: our dirt and our hair, and what was left of the remaining bubbles now gray with our filth. (Not mine, of course. Even AFTER a bath, my bubbles are snowy white. But baths at the orphanage were a "shared experience," and there was dirt aplenty, let me tell you!)

But here's the thing, when I have a nightmare, I see all of the real-life stuff: the pulling of the plug, the rusty grate, the noisy slurps, and the mini tornado of filth and grime ...

Only — and here's the gruesome part — in the dream, my body starts to dissolve, and I become a human Slurpee!

It's gross. I know. And I'm not sure how that would work, exactly. Our bodies don't just DISSOLVE. But if you think about it —

bubbles vaporize or evaporate in the tub, so that was probably my thinking at the time.

And as the dream continues, since I'm basically just human slime at this point, I get SUCKED DOWN THE DRAIN along with the dirty water, and I'm sent out to sea — or Lake Michigan, I guess it would be since I lived in Chicago — where my slushy body mixes with the gross sewage and all the dead goldfish.

And if you're wondering how dead goldfish factor into the story, it's because of Trixie.

(Stay with me for a minute while I take a slight turn in the story.)

We couldn't have dogs or cats at the orphanage for obvious reasons. But we had a small fish tank with a single goldfish, and we named him or her Trixie. (Figuring out a fish's gender is dicey. Trust me on this one.)

Unfortunately, Trixie died of young age and unnatural causes when someone fed him or her an entire box of cornflakes. (Did you know, M, that a goldfish will continue to eat until its intestines rupture?)

We all watched, horrified, the night of Trixie's untimely death as the temporary night aide scooped Trixie from the tank with the net thingy, her lower hand trying to catch the drips, as she marched to the bathroom, and we scrambled to follow, wondering what would happen next.

With wide eyes and breaking hearts, we watched the aide open the toilet lid, and then with a quick flick of her wrist as if she was flipping a pancake with a spatula, the aide turned the net sunny side over, and she plopped Trixie into the toilet, where Trixie landed with a gentle "plink" into the shallow pool of dirty porcelain.

"Swim, Trixie," my little orphan brother, Max, whispered as he bent his head low into the bowl, his tears running down his freckled face and onto Trixie's lifeless body like drops of salty rain.

But we all knew it was hopeless. Trixie's exploded stomach and tiny fish guts told it all.

And then, without so much as a simple prayer for poor Trixie, the aide pulled the chrome handle, and she flushed little Trix down the toilet and into the Metropolitan Water Reclamation District of Greater Chicago.

I wasn't the only one who had flushing nightmares after Trixie left us. Lots of kids did. And the night aide got in trouble from her "poor handling of the situation." I overheard the supervisor say the aide should have had someone run to the pet store and switch dead Trixie with a new live fish while we were sleeping. It didn't have to be an exact replica. Any color was fine. Silver? Speckled? We were only kids, after all. What would we know?

Then she added, "At the very least, you could have replaced Trixie with a goldfish CRACKER. There must be some stale ones around," until they could find a proper substitute.

Oops! I forgot to empty the dishwasher, and my dad is yelling at me from the kitchen.

(OK. It's not really yelling. It's more just like REALLY LOUD voice projection.)

See ya in a few!

W.

WACKY WEDNESDAY, PART 2, 7:25 P.M.

Sorry about that. Not only did I put away the dishes, but I helped myself to some ice cream as a reward for all of my hard work. Yum!!

Now, back to the story, and since I've run a bit off course, let me circle back.

So, anyway, I'd awaken from the drain dream screaming and crying and in a smelly wet puddle of pee — usually mine, but sometimes my bedmate's. (The orphanage where you left me had two and three-fer sleeping accommodations. Two or three orphans "fer" each bed.)

It would take Amy (she was my least favorite permanent night duty aide) an hour or so to calm me down, and Amy would explain that it was PHYSICALLY impossible for my three-year-old body to fit down the two-inch circumference of the drain.

Only Amy didn't use the word "circumference." She used the word "HOLE," saying, "Willa, quit being such a crybaby. Your big body cannot possibly fit down that little two-inch hole. And if you want something to cry about, I'll give you something to cry about. Now go back to sleep."

And then she'd change my wet underwear, but not the sheets, and I'd have to spoon tightly against my bedmate until morning so I wouldn't have to sleep in the wet pee spot.

So Gross!

The drain phobia ended when Ted and Diane Shisbey adopted me the following year, and the stress of the adoption made my hair fall out. (I was super happy to be adopted, but still, it was scary in that "Stranger Danger" sort of way where kids are told to be wary of people they don't know.)

Because of the stress, my thick dark hair started falling out in patches and it clogged the drain in the tub that Olivia (my new bratty adoptive sister) and I shared. Olivia made a humongous deal about it, insisting to her mom, Diane (my new adoptive mom), that I should be "grounded" for losing so much hair and clogging the tub with my "gross orphan hair."

It was then I realized that if MY HAIR couldn't even make it down the drain, my body wouldn't either.

FYI: To cover up the bald spots, Olivia made me wear a tri-colored knit cap with fake locks of hair for three full weeks because, according to her, my balding head was "an embarrassment to the Shisbey name." The joke was on Olivia though, because, believe it or not, I loved that hat. It was super warm, it was colorful, and the locks were fun to "toss." (I'd never had hair that was long enough to toss before.)

Diane made me throw the cap away for reasons I won't go into (but trust me when I say her wording seemed culturally insensitive), and Olivia got grounded because my Dad said her poor treatment of me bordered on emotional torture and he wouldn't tolerate it.

Oopsie!

Now my dad really is hollering at me from the kitchen. I guess I spaced and forgot to put the Ben & Jerry's Chubby Hubby (delish!) back in the freezer, and now there's a melted mess all over the counter.

Bye for now,

Willa

ANOTHER ZOMBIE SLOG DAY, 9:02 P.M.

Dear M,

Tonight my dad and I went out to our favorite pizza restaurant for dinner. Dad said he was too tired to cook. But between you and me, I think he was too GROSSED-OUT. My dad's a dentist, and today he had to pull a bunch of rotten teeth out of a guy's mouth.

According to my dad, the teeth smelled "to the high heavens," which means it can be smelled across great distances. And not to obsess over the guy's rotten teeth odor, but if my dad could smell it through a mask and a face shield, then you know the stench had to be super gnarly.

My dad said he was preparing the guy for something called "dental implants," which are basically false teeth but with a fancy new name. They're drilled into your bones, so you get to keep them in your mouth at night instead of soaking them in a jar on the bathroom counter like they did in the olden days.

While we were at dinner, my dad tried — and he failed —to get me to "open up" about my feelings regarding the divorce.

When my dad asked about my feelings, my mind went foggy and my pizza suddenly tasted like Silly Putty (which is essentially tasteless, as far as flavors go, but which has this cool squishy-ness that squeaks when you bite it. Or so I'm told. Wink wink.)

Believe it or not, M, I'm not good with talking about emotional stuff or sharing my feelings. I can with you, in these diary posts, but not in real life, and ESPECIALLY not when sitting across from the lady who is my new therapist!

Confessions of a Nerdy Girl: Diary #5

Can you believe it? Only 13, and yet I have a shrink. (Although my dad says that the term "shrink" is no longer socially acceptable. Now we're supposed to call them "Stress Management and Family Crisis Counselors.")

It's just that there are so many feelings and words inside of me, and they're all jumbled and mixed together so tightly that I can't get them sorted. It's like a tangled ball of yarn that's all twisted.

No. That's not quite right, because a ball of yarn is one single, although verrrryyyyy long continuous string.

My feelings are complicated. It's like they're part of one emotion and part of another.

So maybe it's more like this: Have you ever left a bag of Sour Gummi Worms in a hot car? And how the sugar-coated, two-tone worms all melt onto one another, and so when you take them out parts of the yellow and green worms blend with the orange and blue ones? Sometimes they can be easily pulled apart, but sometimes part of one worm melts onto another, and it becomes a single ginormous yellow and green and blue combo worm.

OK. I just re-read that, and it's not a very clear analogy, and between the Gummy Worm analogy and the Silly Putty reference, I come off as a kid who definitely needs a shrink! Ugh!!!!!!

What I mean is that sometimes I'm sad, and sometimes I'm angry. And sometimes they both mix together and it becomes something else, a new feeling. Like hopelessness, but a mad hopelessness. And then later, it morphs into a new feeling, like frustration, which leads to anger, which leads to depression because I'm mad that I'm angry.

(Again, I just re-read that last paragraph, and if you can answer the question "Which came first? The chicken or the egg?" you'll be able to figure out what I'm trying to say. Ha!)

And then there are some days, M, where I don't feel ANYTHING at all. Seriously. It's like someone has blown out the candle that lights me.

I'm not happy. I'm not sad. I'm not angry.

Zip.

Instead, I'm a zombie slogging through an endless day.

But then something random will happen, like I'll hear a familiar song, or I'll smell the scent of freshly cut grass, or the tremor from a passing trash truck rumbles down my spine, and it triggers a memory. And because I have that weird disorder, H-SAM, it sucks me back through a time vortex and feelings will start to ooze through the cracks of my time and space continuum. And then, WHAMO! I'm dealing with a whole new mess of emotions from a month, a year, or five years ago!

See what I mean? My feelings are the Sour Gummis! Melting all over each other, creating a messy, gooey gummy soup of "Woe is me." Boo Hoo. Poor Willa. The weird OCD orphan kid who can't keep a mom.

I'm such a loser...

I'm going to end this for now. I'm in the middle of a major pity party, and it's not a party you'd want to attend.

Willa

Confessions of a Nerdy Girl: Diary #5

A BRA STORY, 10:51 P.M.

Dear M,

Therapy is NOT fun! Unless it's shopping therapy. Shopping therapy is a blast.

SHOP TIL YOU DROP

And I am SOOO kidding!!!

I hate shopping. I actually have shopping PHOBIA, and you'd have shopping phobia too if the last two times you went shopping it was with YOUR DAD, and both times it was to get a bra!

No lie. My last shopping experiences were both at a Walmart when my dad had to take me to get my first, AND my second, which might potentially be my last, (if things don't start speeding up) bra.

Usually, Diane and Olivia would shop together for Mother/Daughter time, as they'd call it, Olivia often saying and with a sneer on her face, "ME and MY MOM are having mother/daughter time. Too bad you don't have a mom." (And sorry to say this, M, but if we ever meet or hang out, let's not go shopping, OK? Let's just walk around and talk or something.)

Anyway, if I needed clothes, Diane would get them for me from the boys' section, which is sorta how Diane saw me, as a tomboy, instead of a girly girl. Or as a princess — in Olivia's case, dressed in rainbow sherbet-colored lace and netting and with a fake pink smile drawn on her lips at the plastic factory, where she was molded, packaged, and shipped directly to the Shisbeys' mailbox in a cellophane box.

My Go-To ensembles are T-shirts and jeans, or white button-down shirts if I'm "dressing up," paired with jeans and black and white Converse sneakers on my feet.

But Diane always made my dad take me shopping if I needed something specific, because, in Diane's words, "You brought her home, Ted; it's your responsibility to care for her."

And I know EXACTLY what you're thinking right now. You're thinking the same thing I did when Diane said it. That what she told my dad is a line parents say when they let their kids adopt a DOG FROM THE POUND, not something a mom says to a dad when they adopt a kid from an orphanage.

Whatever, though...

I've heard worse. And as the square peg in the round hole of humanity, I've learned to grow a thick skin.

Now, back to my bra story...

Have you been to a Walmart? (FYI: Know what you CAN'T buy at a Walmart? Walls!! Ha! And yet you CAN buy a real CASKET for your deceased family members! They're not on aisle 4 or anything, but you can order them online according to my dad.)

Anyway, I don't know about YOUR Walmart, but mine has the dressing room in the MIDDLE of the store, not in some far-off obscure corner. And it's not even one with solid walls or anything. This particular dressing room was some pop-up flimsy thing they erected at the last minute.

So, instead of it ("it" being bra shopping with my DAD) being a low-key stealth operation, I was forced to shop in full view of the ENTIRE WORLD, while my dad pulled random bras off the racks and shouted across the aisles at me, "WILLA! ARE YOUR BREASTS BIG ENOUGH FOR A REAL CUP!? OR DO YOU NEED SOMETHING LIKE THIS? SOMETHING CALLED A 'TRAINER'!!?"

Confessions of a Nerdy Girl: Diary #5

while frantically waving over his head what looked to be two tiny white flags, but sewn together in the middle.

I guess my dad didn't know (and why would he?) that I'd been wearing "a trainer" since I was 10 when Diane bought me my first 3-pack, saying it was about time I "covered up the dimes on my ironing board."

"WILLA!" My dad shouted at me a second time, waving his flags again, although this time it was pink and blue polka dots. "HOW'S THIS?! THIS ONE HAS A PATTERN!!" and his tone was far more excited than the situation deserved.

I mumbled something back at him while sorting through a rack with the sign reading "Sports Bras." They seemed more casual-like, without all the lace and molded cups and stuff, and more appropriate for my tomboy chest. But even the sports bras were way too big.

"HONEY!! HOW BIG ARE YOU — WOULD YOU SAY?!!" Dad hollered, his voice sounding more insistent, and holding up a black humongous thing that even Olivia couldn't possibly fill. "GIVE ME AN IDEA!!"

I wasn't sure. Bigger than an acorn at least, but an orchard away from an apple.

Some nice lady with an armful of cotton grannie panties saw my distress, and she went over to my dad and helped him find a few suitable options from the teen section. But unlike the adult bra section, where the colors ranged from the standard white or black, or that weird color someone in the bra-control room thinks is "flesh-tone," (come on, who on earth has skin the color of canned tuna? Like, literally, NO ONE ON THE PLANET!) the teen bra choices leaned more towards colors you'd find in packaged cotton candy at the fairgrounds: bubblegum pink, tangerine orange, limey green, and such.

The bra shopping trauma didn't stop there, with random customers having to come to my aid. It continued when my dad insisted I try them all on, reminding me that's how I wound up with a C-cup bra the first time around. It was because I didn't try it on. Instead, just grabbed the first one I saw. (Olivia inherited that one, and it fit her perfectly.)

"We have three BRAS!" my dad said to the dressing room assistant, and I'm pretty sure the added volume on the word "bras" was intentional and for my added embarrassment.

The lady counted the bras, "One ... Two ... Three ..." she droned tonelessly, bored out of her gourd, and then she handed them back to my dad along with a plastic circle with the number 3 on it.

My dad practically had to push me through the dressing room door because my feet were glued to the floor as dread and humiliation ran from the tips of my unpainted toenails to the top of my dandruff-filled head.

Technically it's "dry scalp," but Olivia says it's dandruff. She also said that once I get acne — she insists it will happen — I'll hit what is known as the **Loser Trifecta**: Acne, Dandruff, and Glasses. And once I gain 20 pounds — which Olivia also insists will happen — I'll hit the Quadfecta, which is the loserest of losers. (FYI: There's a strong chance Olivia is betting on horse races, because Olivia is not smart enough to know the definition of trifecta, or that quad comes after tri).

I unglued my feet once I realized my dad was standing in the bra department, in a store my classmates might shop in, and holding onto my potential new undergarments, which was BEYOND awkward!!

AWKWARD

"You go inside and try them on, and I'll be just outside the door. Here!" My dad pointed to the floor. "In case you need help with..." He looked down at the bras he held in his hand and then at my chest, and his face flushed with embarrassment. "With, whatever," he finished, handing me the bunch of bras still attached to the hangers and gently pushing me through the dressing room door.

Once inside the small stark cubicle with a full-length and spit-covered mirror, (Or snot. Maybe it was kid snot, cuz it was at the bottom, at kid-nose level) I froze. Not from cold, even though it was cold in the store, I froze from anxiety because my dad was standing so close to the door that I could see his shoes from under that lame half-door.

"Uh, Dad?" I said.

"Yes, Willa?"

"Could you, like, back up or something, please? I need my space. This is awkward enough without you standing right outside the door."

"Oh! Sure. Sorry," he said, and I watched as his feet receded from my view, his shoes making squeaky sounds while I counted to 10 to keep myself from hyperventilating.

Seriously, M, if I hadn't just come from therapy, I would have needed to GO TO therapy. That's how freaked I was about the whole deal.

Plus... do you know what I found out when trying on real bras?

Unlike my trainers, which are a cinch to put on — just pulling them on over my head like a T-shirt — cup bras are SUPER tricky! And I didn't research this or anything, but I'm convinced that they must have been invented by a man because if a woman designed them they would NOT have those lame hook and eye closures on the BACK of the bra where you can't even reach. I'm sure a woman would have designed the closure on the FRONT. Plus, it wouldn't be a hook and eye at all, it would be a zipper! Or maybe snaps or something. Don't ya think?

So anyway, there I was, inside the sorta, kinda, almost, dressing room, fumbling around and forced to look in the mirror at my gross bare white skin and goosebumps (and I mean my actual flesh, not my two... uh ... you-know-whats or my "dimes" as Diane called them) with my dad on the other side of the door sounding like a deranged cheerleading and yelling out random stuff.

"YOU GOOD?"

"YOU CAN DO THIS!"

"WILLA, HOW'S THE FIT?"

"HONEY! DO YOU NEED A HAND?"

I don't know about a hand, but what I could have used was two longer arms, because I could NOT get the hook and eyes to catch! I practically pulled my arms out of their sockets trying to reach around to the middle of my back. Two different rows of hook choices and yet I couldn't seem to get one single hook out of six to attach.

My shoulders hurt, my neck ached, and my fingers were cramping.

"HELLO? SWEETIE??... DO YOU NEED ME TO COME IN AND HELP?"

(Come in and help?? Was he joking??)

In frustration, I pulled off the bra, took a deep breath, and I said to myself, "What would Sheldon do?"

Now, before you get too weirded-out, let me explain.

Sheldon is a fictional character from my favorite TV show, "The Big Bang Theory." Sheldon is super smart (he's an astrophysicist), and like me, Sheldon has OCD. Unlike me, Sheldon would have first assessed the variables of the situation and proceeded using basic logic.

So that's what I did. I used logic.

I discovered that if you attach the bra around your chest with the back to the front first, without putting your arms through the straps, you can then twist the bra back around and stick your arms through the straps after. Then you just need to adjust the straps by tightening them at the clip part, which you need to do, or the bra just sags as if it's just too tired or bored to stay upright.

I also had some trouble figuring out the proper "fit" part of the process, meaning, how to tell if it was my perfect size. (I gotta say, M, it would have been nice to have a mom right about then.)

My confusion about the fit was that I wasn't sure if I needed to use the same rule for bras that is used for shoes.

You know the shoe rule, right? How you're supposed to leave a thumb's length of empty shoe at the tip of a new shoe so there's room to grow? (I'm sure you've had the shoe salesmen do that before, when they fit you for shoes. How the guy or girl leans down and presses their thumb on the tip of the shoe to feel where your toes are.)

Well, that's what I did, except the bra version. I left a thumb's width of space in my bra to allow for breast growth. (Truth be told, it was more like TWO thumb's worth. I'm nothing if not optimistic! Ha!)

BUT...

Come to find out, the thumb rule does NOT apply to bras according to Olivia. (Olivia is a bit of a boob and bra expert, or so she claims, because, according to her, she has an "ample bosom" and has worn a bra since she was like 9 or something.)

Olivia also told me that I had to be the dumbest orphan sister alive when I went in her room to show her my new bras. (This happened P.D. ... Pre-divorce, when she still lived at the house and terrorized me 24/7.)

Olivia had gotten off of her bed to come to the door so she could nag at me up close. (Interesting Fact: I've NEVER been allowed to cross the threshold and enter Olivia's "Inner Sanctum," as she calls her room. Although "The Devil's Lair" is a more accurate description.)

"Have you NOT seen a Victoria's Secret catalogue, Willa?" she said. "The point of a bra is to OVERFILL it, not underfill it." She jabbed her finger twice on my flat chest. "That's just bra one-oh-one, nerd nugget. You always need to buy a bra that's at least a size smaller than you need so you can spill over the top of it. Like this." And then she embarrassed the snot out of me by pulling up her shirt to show me her barely covered ta-tas. (And proving beyond a doubt that Olivia practices what she preaches because her bra barely covers her dimes!)

A couple days later, my dad exchanged the bras for a smaller size, so things worked out OK in the end.

Until next time,

Your Once Upon a Time daughter,

Willa

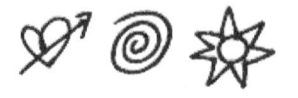

WILLA RAMBLINGS, 10:13 A.M.

Dear M,

I've been giving a lot of thought lately about the saying, "The apple doesn't fall far from the tree."

I'm sure you've heard that particular "golden oldie" as my dad calls all the corny sayings that he's so fond of using once or twice, or a million times. But just in case you don't have a dad like mine who uses language not heard since the 1920s, that particular saying means that the kid — who is supposed to be the apple — shows similar qualities and behaviors to those of their parents — the tree.

It's like how if a parent has a talent for music then the kid might have music talent too, or if the parent is super smart, then the kid has a good shot at going to Harvard or Yale. (Or wherever it is that smart kids go to college these days).

But science proves in the "Nature versus Nurture" debate that it's not always genetics that makes us who we are. Sometimes we become the way we are because of how we're raised. Like, how if a kid is raised with wolves, the kid becomes wolfish. (Or I guess it would be "wolf-like.")

KIDDING!!

I am SO kidding. (Although if you've ever seen or read "The Jungle Book," you'll know that a kid raised by animals isn't just your average kid.)

I've been wondering if I'm the way that I am (with my OCD and my H-SAM) because I'm a part of you, gene-wise, or if it's my life's experiences that have made me who — and WHAT — I am.

That's the thing with being adopted: there are so many QUESTIONS that circle around in my head.

And just so you know, the questions don't circle around in an orderly fashion, one after the other, like kids holding hands in a ring-around-the-rosie.

Instead, it's more like the questions are a swarm of gnats that have disturbed a swarm of bees, and so it's a turf war with my head as the turf, and the insects are all buzzing and fighting and making me crazy.

Don't get me wrong, it's not as if I'm looking to BLAME someone for who I am, but it would be nice not to have to take 100% responsibility for my non-normalness.

Now that you know a little more about me, are you aware of any similarities between us? Like, do you also count the cracks in the sidewalk when you're out for a stroll? (It's actually sort of fun.) Or align your stuffed animals by size and color and touch each one on the head before you go to bed at night? (Cuz it's actually quite calming.) Or collect certain things? (As I've mentioned before, my curated favorites include novelty erasers, calendars, and gum wrappers. But not just any kind of gum wrapper. Only the silver foil ones that you can make things out of, like rings and stuff.)

Or, if I'm not like you, am I like my birth father? Or do you have other kids besides me, and maybe I'm like them, another brown-eyed, brown-haired hottie, perhaps? Ha!! Or if you don't have any other kids, do I share similarities with YOUR siblings (assuming you have some) or your parents?

By my calculations, you're in your 30s now, so my guess is that my "gram gram" and "paw paw" are still living. (And I'm joking with that gram gram stuff. Kids in California don't go for those cutesy names. They just pretty much stick with Grandma and Grandpa.)

But that brings up another issue of mine (of which there seem to be many!) Sometimes a person can be labeled something in relationship to us, and then the label changes. Are you still my mom because you gave birth to me? Or did you stop being my mom once you walked down the steps from Children's Home Society of Chicago and away from me all of those years ago?

This divorce deal is also super complicated. Will my family still be my family? I mean, I know my dad will stay my dad (hopefully!!) but is

Diane still my adoptive mom? Or does she become my adoptive mom once-removed? And is Olivia Shisbey still my adoptive sister? (Not sure I'm gonna cry many tears over that one if the answer is NO.)

I don't understand how I legally became a Shisbey with the drop of the judge's gavel (I'm exaggerating. He signed a paper. There wasn't any gavel pounding.), and now my dad and Diane will be granted a divorce in much the same way to dissolve the marriage. But does the family DISSOLVE too?

I asked my dad to explain things to me and he said, (in a cranky voice) "Willa, you know about as much as I know. I promise you that we will always be a family. And, just so we're clear, Diane can no more relinquish your affiliation and legal status as her daughter as she can unbirth Olivia!"

He sort of yelled it, so it sounded as if he was trying to convince himself. Plus, his explanation was a bit of a "word salad" (a jumble of incoherent speech). But I got what he was saying, that legally I would remain Diane's daughter forever, much to her displeasure I'm sure. (And I don't know about you, but the unbirthing Olivia part is sort of yucky if you picture the visual of how that would even work.)

Ewww...

Hopefully, my dad gets to keep our house so we can stay here in Huntington Beach, especially since my dad's dental practice is nearby. But divorce is a "COMPLICATED THING," according to my dad, and it has a lot of "MOVING PARTS," and the husband usually "GETS THE SHORT END OF THE STICK."

If we have to sell the house, my dad says we'll get a two-bedroom apartment, but then I'd have to move away from my BFF Marley Applegate, and that's even way worse than my dad and Diane divorcing.

As I'm finding out, divorce might seem easy peasy lemon breezy, but it's not. There's a lot of harsh words that occur because of it. (Along with a few bad ones. You wouldn't believe the words I heard Olivia say when Diane told her they were moving to the East Coast. Especially when Olivia found out the weather is so cold that she'll have to wear baggy clothes like sweaters and coats that don't show off her cute figure.)

If I tell you a secret, M, will you promise not to judge me? And I know that what I'm about to say makes me a terrible, horrible, awful person, but here it is:

I WISHED THE DIVORCE INTO EXISTENCE.

I know it's horrible, but it's true.

It's just that I got so **WEARY** of the mean way that Diane and Olivia treated me all of these years. The things they would say, or do, and the constant exclusion from all the fun stuff. (It's not like I **WANTED** to have a mani/pedi, but it would have been nice to have been asked to come along. And so maybe my dark brown hair doesn't need dying at the salon, but I could have had my ends trimmed or something while Olivia and Diane had their highlights.)

So I wished them away, thinking that I wasn't really a **TOTALLY** bad person, because I was only wishing for a divorce, (which has a 50/50 chance of happening anyway.) It's not like I was wishing for something bad to happen to them. (Well, except for me wishing that Olivia would get cystic acne and Diane would grow facial hair that normal waxing wouldn't solve.)

It's just that I love my dad so much that I didn't want to share him. (I'm selfish that way.) And I know that he loves me a lot too. And not in a "he feels sorry for me" kind of way because of how I looked before he helped with my surgery to fix my messed up face from my cleft lip, or how I had a crooked eyeball behind those goggle glasses I wore, and how no one else wanted me because I wasn't considered "cute" by today's standards (or ANY standards, really).

Wishing it was just my dad and me wasn't my only wish either. There were lots that were equally, if not more, important. (When you're me, there are SO MANY things that need to be wished into place!) So I've been pretty busy throughout my life using birthday candle wishes, shooting star wishes, and pennies-into-wells wishes, wishing for other things too ...

Things like...

I wish I was normal.

I wish kids liked me.

I wish I was pretty.

I wish I had smaller: Feet. Nose. Ears...

I wish you never gave me up for adoption.

But like I said, there were lots of times where I wished really hard that it was just my dad and me living by ourselves and that the mother-daughter duo would just evaporate...

Poof! Into thin air.

Or teleport to another dimension.

As I got older, I realized my Star Trek version of their disappearance was farfetched — not to mention dangerous — because some of those other planets were super deadly. And the wish became simpler, that Diane and Olivia would pack the car with all of their silly designer clothing and stuff and drive off and never come back. (But maybe leave behind a forwarding address in case we wanted to send them a Christmas or a birthday card on occasion.)

And that's why now I'm super confused about my feelings. How maybe it really is all my fault, despite my dad saying otherwise...

Yours in confusion and teenage angst,

Willa

SOME DOOZIE NEWSIE, 6:24 P.M.

Dear M,

I have some MAJOR news, and I'm not sure yet if the news is good news, bad news, or maybe it's just "News." (I'll come to a proper judgement of it eventually.)

NEWS

Today my dad surprised me with my first major pet! I say "major pet" because the only other pets I've had have been fish, and they both exploded, as you'll recall.

I know, right? What's up with that??

R I P

You'd think I would have learned NOT to overfeed a fish after the Trixie debacle at the orphanage, but nooooo! Instead, I managed to balloon-pop my own little guy (gal?) that my dad gave me when I was 7, by overfeeding it fish flakes. Which oddly enough are flakes that are made OUT of fish FOR fish. (And it's a good thing us humans haven't yet caught on to this gross practice!)

Dad won the goldfish for me at a local carnival by tossing a ping pong ball into the center of a fishbowl. It wasn't an empty bowl. It was half-filled with some water and it had a fake goldfish lolling about on the bottom.

The game sounds easy to do; just aim and toss a little ball. But it's not. Because the water acts like a trampoline and it makes the ball bounce OUT of the bowl. That's assuming the ball actually makes it INSIDE the bowl in the first place. (And it doesn't; instead, it hits the carnival guy right between the eyes with a loud BOINK and then bounces off his head and into the deep fryer at Hot Dog on a Stick, the next stand over.)

Everyone gets three tries for their 20 bucks or whatever that it cost to play. My dad aced it on his third toss, so he won the prize: A Fish-in-a-Baggie! (With a value of about 50 cents, including the baggie, and assuming the water was free.)

I'm not sure why you don't win the bowl and the fake fish.

Instead, you win a REAL goldfish, struggling to swim in two inches of water and gasping for air inside a tightly knotted baggie. Then, because the clock is ticking before your Fish-in-a-Baggie suffocates, or you drop it on the ground where it explodes like a water balloon at a 5-year-old's birthday party, your parents are forced to rush to the pet store to "spend a fortune" as Diane complained, buying a fishbowl, some colored pebbles that look like Pop Rocks, and a teeny tiny underwater playground, because, according to my dad, "Even fish need daily exercise." (WHAT???? Isn't swimming, like, EXERCISE??)

Anyway. After I killed poor "Fish" (Yes, I named him Fish. I figured not having a real name would make it easier on me when he died, and that probability was high), the horror stayed with me for a while, so I never really wanted another pet.

And so, what a BIG SURPRISE, when lo and behold, my dad walks through the door of the house with a new pet to fill the place my heart used to be. Because that's what you do when the family implodes because of a divorce — you fill it with gifts and pets and trips to the ice cream shop.

Just WHAT KIND of pet did your dad give you, you ask?

Perhaps a cute dog to play with? One that's unconditionally loving and likes to lick the salt off your skin?

Or how about a fluffy cat who will give you side glances and stink-eye like a bored teen, just because that's what cats do?

Or maybe a tiny little hamster in a cage with one of those cute little Ferris wheel things and some shredded wood clippings lining the bottom of it that smell like the inside of Diane's coat closet? (Cedar wood, I think.)

Nope. Nope. And nope.

Are you ready for this one?

My new pet is a PARROT!!

And not some glorious specimen of a parrot with clear eyes and a smooth beak and covered in shiny feathers of green and yellow. Instead, my parrot has gray cloudy eyes with goop at the corners, a crusty chipped beak that looks like an old man's yellowed toenail, and more pink scabby bald spots than it has feathers. (I think it's call "mange," and it's from having "mites," which are bugs. BUGS!!!!)

Basically, my dad has gifted me a million-year-old, mangy, mite-infested parrot with cataracts. What's not to love? Right?

The parrot is a HIM, and his name is REGINALD. He came pre-named, because you can't live to be a million and remain nameless.

And so yeah, Reginald may be the ugliest parrot on the planet and smell like a forgotten wet moldy sock found at the bottom of a gym locker the last day of the school year, but he has a super duper funny and amazing talent!

Are you ready for it?

He TALKS!!

Yeah, I know. Duh! That's not necessarily a news flash because parrots are known for their "verbal abilities." (And their really cool nut-cracking skills. You should see Reg crack open a peanut! It's a site to behold.)

But Reginald doesn't just everyday talk in everyday language. No! My parrot speaks STEWIE!!

In case you're not familiar, Stewie is a fictional character on an animated, not-meant-for-kids, TV series (whose title will remain unspoken, because then I'd have to admit that I've accidentally seen this "trash" as Diane calls it, when I happened by Olivia's room on a couple of occasions.) Stewie is flamboyant, eccentric, rude, and he has a mastery of physics and mechanical engineering that's hi-fi science fiction level.

Oh! And did I mention that Stewie is a one-year-old infant? LOL. That's showbiz for ya!

Anyway, obviously my parrot was a big fan of the show, and so now I own a parrot who shouts out random rude stuff that he learned from Stewie. "What the deuce?" and

"Buttscratcher! Buttscratcher!" seem to be a couple of his favorites. (There's a couple of other doozies, but then both Stewie and I are going to get our mouths "washed out by soap" according to my dad if we repeat them.)

Right now Reginald has to sleep in my dad's bedroom because there's a strong chance I'm highly allergic to him. But Dad says to give it a few days, and that if I don't go into anaphylactic shock and stop breathing, then we're good to go, and Reggie can sleep in my room.

Yay! (And you can't hear me, but that is a totally sarcastic yay. The bird has bugs and he smells. I sort of hope that I AM allergic so that he can stay in my dad's room.)

XOXO,

Willa

AKA: The Fish Terminator

SUNLESS SUNDAY, 8:08 P.M.

Dear M,

Sometimes being a kid is hard work. Not hard work like what my dad does as a dentist each day, filling cavities or pulling rotten teeth or whatever.

The hard work that I'm talking about is more EMOTIONAL than physical.

And I'm not alone. My friends don't have an easy time of it either. Take Marley, my bestie. Marley is as good as they get. She's sweet. She's generous. And she's super smart. And I mean SUPER smart! Like rocket scientist smart or robotic brain surgery smart. Marley is also the editor of our school paper and loved by ALMOST everyone she meets, but it's not a solid 100 percent.

You see, M, Marley's dad, is white (well, I guess technically he's considered "Caucasian," in that "check the box" kind of way, but in real life, he has a dark tan because he's a surfer) and Marley's mom is Jamaican (with a super cool accent!). Unlike my old school in Chicago, where we had lots of kids whose parents were born in other parts of the world, there's not a ton of diversity at Triton Middle School, so Marley's brown skin is the exception rather than the rule.

I don't know why it should make one bit of difference how much pigment or melanin someone has in their skin, but it does, and so sometimes kids say mean things behind Marley's back. I've even heard kids call her Chocolate Chip (not to her face, because, like I said, Marley is the editor of the school paper, and you don't want to anger someone who wields "the power of the pen," and who has the ability to print a really bad picture of you in the school paper).

And what's with Chocolate Chip anyway? Everyone knows that chocolate chips are a super delish mini treat that melts in your mouth in an explosion of creamy sweetness. But leave it to the brats at Triton to take something good and make it into a racial slur.

Marley insists that it doesn't bother her when the kids say mean things, that it says more about THEM than it does about her. Marley says there are more important things for her to worry about — things like famine, global warming, and a widening political divide. But I can tell when Marley's sad because her body curves itself into a comma, and she gets quiet, and so I know that someone has said something that hurts her.

💔 💔 💔

And then there's my new friend Sam, who's had a REALLY tough time of things. Sam's mom died of cancer and her dad lost his job. (I think he got fired because he had to take off a bunch of time from work to care for Sam's mom.) And because they didn't have the money to pay the rent on their house, they got kicked out, and so Sam and her dad and her brother had to live in their crummy old van.

Like, literally live INSIDE it. Sleeping, eating, and doing homework and stuff. How sad is that, right?

Well it put a stop to my little pity party, I'll tell you, when I found out that my new friend didn't have a real house to live in. Plus, the van didn't even have a bathroom or a shower! I'm not sure where they went to do their "business," as my dad calls it. (I was too embarrassed to ask.) But I know that Sam and her brother made sure to shower at P.E., because it would be the only shower they'd get. (Her dad showered at the YMCA, she said.)

Sam told me that her homeless experience helped to put a positive spin on the single GROSSEST thing about school life: Showering at P.E. — because NO KID IN THE

UNIVERSE WANTS TO TAKE SCHOOL SHOWERS!!

Unless, of course, you happen to live in your car, and then you realize it's either a school shower or NO shower!

Suddenly, an over-chlorinated drizzle of lukewarm water coming from a rusty overhead nozzle, and using a pretzel-smelling, crispy towel the size of a paper napkin to dry with is better than no shower at all.

I'll tell you a little bit more about Sam and how she came to be my friend the next time I write to you. Right now I have to go. I hear my dad rummaging around in the garage, which means he's cleaning again and throwing out boxes of Olivia's junk, and I don't want him to accidentally throw my stuff away.

And by "stuff," I mean my collection of fast food wrappers.

I know it's hard to believe, but I'd never eaten "fast food" from a "drive-thru" before I came to live with the Shisbeys. (Orphanage kids don't get out much.) So the fact that I got to drive up in a CAR and order off a HUGE illuminated menu with not only tons of food CHOICES, but also with so many different OPTIONS like:

With cheese or without?

Ketchup or mustard? (Or ketchup AND mustard?)

Lettuce and/or pickles?

Toasted bun or soft?

Grilled onions?

Fresh onions? No onions?

Large fries or small?

Coke?

Root beer?

Sprite?

Mountain Dew? (Small/Medium/Large?)

Vanilla Shake?

Chocolate Shake? ...

— Well, as you can imagine, it was pretty AMAZING!

Actually, it was better than amazing, but I can't quite come up with a more amazing word than amazing. And so, for the first couple of years, I kept the wrappers. (Don't worry. I washed and dried them before I stored them.)

I have In-N-Out Burger Double-Double wrappers, some wrappers from Whoppers, Big Mac wrappers, a few Quarter Pounders wrappers, some Dave's Doubles wrappers, and two Wendy's Baconators, plus, I have a bunch of assorted fry envelopes. I tried to keep the soda cups too, but my dad said, "Honey, now you're just being ridiculous."

Yours in goofiness,

Willa

WHINY WEDNESDAY, 4:22 P.M.

Dear M,

I think you'll get a kick out of the story of how Sam and I became friends. On the other hand, you might not, and for reasons you'll see in a bit. But here goes.

I met Sam when she sat down at the empty seat next to me in my Life Science class. I liked her from the first minute I met her because she was dressed in an army jacket and she wore combat boots, and so it was obvious that, like me, she didn't give a nickel about "fashion."

Sam joined our class the same day Miss Meek our teacher, assigned a special project called "Baby Think It Over." It was part of a "life preparedness" effort to give students a taste of what's really in store for us as adults when and IF we choose to have a child.

Confessions of a Nerdy Girl: Diary #5

The project gave us a life-sized fake baby to take care of for 72 consecutive hours. If we responded to the baby's needs successfully (as monitored by its internal sensor), we passed. If we didn't properly respond, we failed. (Do you want to guess how many kids passed? Let me put it this way; you won't need fingers and toes to count! LOL.)

At first, it sounded super lame — getting graded on something as dumb as caring for a fake baby — but if you really think about it, the chances of needing baby care skills at some point in the future is a lot more likely than the need to evaluate expressions, write equations, graph functions, and solve quadratics, (my current Algebra struggles), so there's that.

$(a+b)^2 = a^2 + 2ab + b^2$ $(a+b)^2 = a^2 + 2ab + b^2$

In case you're wondering, the baby wasn't a robot, although that would have been super cool! Instead, the baby was made out of this super soft "latex" (a fancy word for rubber) and looked and felt TOTALLY real! (So real, it was sort of freaky, to be honest.) The babies had different features and skin tones, and some were boys, and some were girls. (Which we quickly discovered with the first diaper change!)

We had to wear these sensor bracelets on our wrists that looked like watches and were electronically synched to our baby. Anyone who removed their wristband or tampered with the electronics inside the baby would signal a "systems shutdown," and the student would receive an automatic F. And after 23 electronic signals of abuse ("Abuse?" We weren't even sure what that meant at the time, but boy did we learn!) or lack of response on our parts, the baby would shut down, also resulting in a fail.

When our baby cried because he or she wanted to be fed or whatever (and there were LOTS of "whatevers"), we would touch our sensor to the baby's heart to stop the crying, then we had to figure out exactly WHY the baby cried in the first place and try to fix the problem because if we didn't, the baby would just keep crying, and according to Miss Meek, we were not to "lose our noodle," but, instead, we needed to just "deal with it."

Whhhhhh!!!

And oh boy! Fixing the problem was a lot harder than it sounds because, duh, it's not like the baby could talk and tell us what was wrong.

Did the baby need a diaper change?

Was it hungry?

Did it need to be burped?

Was it too cold?

Too hot?

Was it just bored?

Or did it just want to annoy us in some passive-aggressive way so that we couldn't get our homework done or use the bathroom or sleep for more than 2 hours straight in the night?

All the information was sent to Miss Meek's computer from each baby's heart monitor. It recorded the time it took us to respond to the first cry and how long it took us to "soothe" the baby. And it was not always a slam-dunk, if you know what I mean. Did you know that there are times when no matter what you do, a baby just wants to cry?

And cry.

And cry.

And cry...

Andromeda, my kid, (Sam named her. Strange name, I know, but who am I to judge?) didn't cry as much as some babies, but, WOW, some of my classmate's babies practically cried for 72 hours straight! And I have to say, M, that if people knew how much trouble it is to take care of a baby, they probably wouldn't have one.

The whole experience gave me a better understanding of why you might have left me at the orphanage. Was I still as annoying at 1 as when I was a newborn? Is that why you left me the day after my first birthday?

Miss Meek told us that our baby's "settings" were at Newborn, so they were going to cry a ton and need constant care, but that as real babies get older, they aren't so "needy."

I'm not sure that Miss Meek knows this for sure because what she refers to as "her kids" are actually her cats (Eenie, Meenie & Miney ... or maybe it's Meenie, Miney & Mo, I forget), and I don't think that cats need — or want — much fussing over them.

Miss Meek gave us our babies on a Friday afternoon and we gave them back on Monday morning. (I know it doesn't sound that long, but trust me, it felt like TEN lifetimes!) We got to trade off with our partner each night, so it gave the other person a chance to eat and sleep and go to the bathroom in peace.

Since there weren't enough babies for everyone to have their own, Miss Meek did this dumb boy/girl pairing of couples as "parents" so we could share a baby and work on "interpersonal relationships," which, as you probably know, means a social connection or affiliation between two people. Only thing is, we were short two boys, so Sam and I were paired.

Which was fine... until...

WHINY WEDNESDAY CONT., 4:27 P.M.

Whoopsie!

Sorry about the "cliffhanger," but nature called, and when you gotta go, you gotta go! Ha!

Anyway, as I was saying...

Sam and I were paired, which I knew meant would increase the level of bullying that I get on a daily basis — BIG TIME!

And sure enough. Because Dakota Duncan, whose level of diabolical makes Olivia's look like preschool playground stuff, cemented it by having her dad call the school and INSIST that if we were going to be pretend parents, then we needed to be pretend married and have a pretend wedding.

And not because Dakota gives two figs about standard practices regarding marriage first and kids second, but because Dakota wanted a chance to pretend-marry Cody Cassidy (my friend, AND THE CUTEST BOY ON THE PLANET!), who was her original partner, and so Dakota could buy a real wedding dress for her pretend wedding to her pretend boyfriend.

We even had the pretend wedding ceremony in class, if you can believe it! It was all sooooo lame.

In the end, Dakota's plan failed when Cody refused to marry her. Cody took one look at Dakota arriving at school and getting out of her dad's car wearing a real-life white wedding dress complete with a veil and train (I think that long part of a veil that drags at the back is called a "train") and he refused to marry her. Cody said he'd rather take an F and fail Science than marry Dakota.

So instead, Dakota had to marry Dylan, which she was pretty mad about because she's known Dylan since they were like 5 or so, and she couldn't get past the fact that Dylan was a major nose-picker in elementary school. (But he was a nose-picker-**flicker**, not a booger-eater like the other nose pickers, so he wasn't quite as gross.)

The project was super emotional for me on lots of different levels, and I cried more than once (but maybe it was the lack of sleep that made me extra weepy and ugly cry for an hour straight on day two). The experience taught me how HARD it is to care for a baby, and so I thought A LOT about you and your choice to leave me at the orphanage. I pictured me as a baby and crying 24/7 and you getting to the end of your rope and wanting to be free of me.

Confessions of a Nerdy Girl: Diary #5

Believe me, there were times when I couldn't get Andromeda to stop crying, and if there was an orphanage nearby, I might have been tempted to drop her off. (Probably not for good, but at least for a few hours so I could take a nap.)

But here's a confession, and it's a doozie!

I did something way, way worse than leaving my child at an orphanage in the care of trained professionals.

Instead ...

(And you are NOT going to believe what a terrible person I am.)

Are you ready for it??

Here goes ...

I LEFT MY BABY ON A CITY BUS!!

I'll repeat that: A. CITY. BUS.

Confessions of a Nerdy Girl: Diary #5

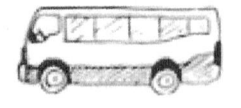

It was a TOTAL ACCIDENT!! But, as it's been pointed out to me now many times and by a million people, if my H-SAM allows for total recall of my life, it should never have happened, right?

Well, yes and no.

OBVIOUSLY, it should NOT have happened! I mean, what kind of nitwit leaves a baby on one of the grossest and dirtiest forms of mass transit? (Second only to a New York City subway car or maybe Chicago's L train.)

But in my defense, the M in H-SAM stands for "Memory," which means I can recall things AFTER THE FACT. When I left Andromeda on the bus, I was still in real-time. Plus, I had a lot on my mind. (Not that that's an excuse or anything.)

As my dad says, finding Andromeda was a "madcap adventure" for sure. (Madcap means zany and ridiculous, I'm sure you know. :-)

But, as luck would have it, Cody — who's known me to wear my pajama pants to school (ONCE) because I somehow forgot to change out of them and into my jeans, and who three times has found my glasses for me, (which were on top of my head at the time) put an electronic tracker inside my baby (without my knowledge or consent, I might add).

Cody said he did it "just in case" my baby got abducted, but he was just saying that to be nice. Cody did it because he knows how absent-minded I can be sometimes. He uses a tracker for his skateboards because his last two were stolen right out of his backpack at lunchtime, so he figured, why not?

Well, let me tell you, I don't know if our adventure was "madcap," like my dad said, but it was crazy, to be sure. The baby napper took Andromeda to Disneyland! Yes, Disneyland, which is not the Happiest Place on Earth when you're trying to find a kid, probably strapped inside a stroller among 40,000 other people, most of who have a kid strapped inside a stroller.

And just as we — Cody, Marley, Sam, Kevin (Sam's brother and our driver), and I were zeroing in on her signal inside Disneyland, the tracker had Andromeda headed OUT of the park, where we followed the signal to a POLICE STATION!

Yes. You read that correctly. A police station! (And don't believe that lame "TO PROTECT AND SERVE" police motto, because the only thing the officer we spoke to wanted to serve — was his mouth — and with a powdered donut.)

That clown thought it was funny that he TRASHED my child.

And I don't mean that he TRASH "TALKED" her — like he called her ugly or something. I mean, he literally ditched her in the dumpster along with the uneaten portion of his pastrami on rye or whatever it was that he had for lunch. And worse, the trash truck had already come, headed for a waste transfer station (where they separate the trash from the recyclables, I think.)

Andromeda was just INCHES away from being pulverized to a pulp by a tractor before I — like any loving Tiger Mom would do — jumped into a Matterhorn-sized pile of hot, smelly, decomposing mess of trash to save her.

And it wasn't just your regular household trash, like rinsed-out Niblets corn cans and the semi-clean paper towels because you pulled off one too many kind. But the horrible dumpster trash stuff!

I was literally sifting through a sea of flattened cat carcasses and decomposing road kill. Stinking blue baggies, squishy and warm with dog poo. Five-gallon white buckets full of wormy-looking cow guts... (At least it looked like cow guts. Gosh. I HOPE it was cow and not leftover surgery parts from the hospital!) Bags and baskets and bundles of the grossest, most disgusting things you can ever imagine! And I fished my child's grimy body out from beneath the huge disgusting mound — JUST IN THE NICK OF TIME!

The things a mother will do for her kid! Am I right???

In the end, it all worked out OK. And with my friends' help, I learned the true meaning of the word "Family" (which I've really been struggling with since the whole divorce deal, and that I'll share with you another time).

But right now, it's getting late, and reliving the trash episode has made me itchy, and I really, really, really need to take a shower just to wash off the memory.

Yours in maternal simpatico,

Willa

IN MEMORIUM: RIP REGGIE, 9:21 P.M.

Dear M,

I am SOOOOOOOOOOO sad.

Reginald died.

And I think I killed him!

I'm a TERRIBLE mom! First with Andromeda, and now with Reginald...

I'M A MOMSTER!!

MOMSTER!

I forgot to give him water. (It was just ONE time. And only for A DAY, but still.) And not only that, but I covered his cage with a towel (to keep his mites from jumping on me while I slept), so there's also a chance I suffocated him too. (Although my dad says you're SUPPOSED to cover birds at night.)

I feel terrible, and I just can't stop crying. (At some point, shouldn't your eyes just run out of water?) If I didn't have my friends to help me through this, I don't know what I'd do.

Death is a complicated and confusing thing for a kid to deal with — whether it's the death of a friend, a family member, OR a pet, but having someone to cry with (like my bestie, Marley) helps.

Dad tried to console me by saying Reggie was probably sick and "on his way out" when my dad bought him, and that's why he was "On Sale" as the "Daily Special" at the pet store.

% OFF

Dad put his arm around my shoulders, he squeezed me, and he said, "Wills, I should have known something was wrong when the darn cage cost me more than the bird," and he sort of chuckled when he said it. (And I don't want to harp on my dad, but Dad could use a little bereavement training on how to console a 13-year-old daughter after her beloved pet passes on to parts unknown.)

But even though it's true that Reggie was old and half-blind, and probably had bird dementia or whatever, and, according to Cody, probably already had "one scabby foot in the grave and a banana peel on the other," Reggie died while in my care.

Ahhhhhh!

What is WRONG with me that I can't keep fish or birds alive? Two pets that rank pretty low when it comes to maintenance. Maybe I wasn't born with the "Maternal Gene" or "Mom Genes" or whatever. (Not to be confused with Mom "**Jeans**," which are these super unflattering and high-waisted jeans that some moms like to wear.)

Is being a good mom a genetic thing, do you think? Is it something that some girls just ARE or are destined to become, even if it's too early for us to use the skill, but how we'll be naturally great at it when the time is right? Or is it something that we all must LEARN, like when we're taught to play the piano, and how there are some girls who are "naturals" and they learn quickly, while for others, three years later, they're still banging on the keys like they're pounding clay?

Maybe it's sort of like that. Some girls are naturally good at mothering and some aren't.

Do we share the "aren't" part? And maybe that's why I'm so crummy at it, and you thought that you were crummy at it too, and so maybe that's why you gave me away? (Inquiring minds want to know.)

But with Reginald's passing, it has me wondering about what happens AFTER. You know, like, the heaven stuff.

Do ALL pets go to heaven? Or is it just dogs?

I ask because there are A LOT of movies about dogs going to heaven! Case in point: "All Dogs Go To Heaven" (1 & 2), "A Dog's Journey," "A Dog's Purpose," "A Dog's Promise," "A Dog's Way Home," "Angel Dog," …

Dog … Dog … Dog …

See a pattern here? Not a single mention of a parrot! So it seems pretty certain (especially if you listen to "The Media") that admission to heaven is limited to humans and/or dogs.

And MAYBE ...

Just maybe ... a few **extra-special** cats. (Seeing-Eye cats or something. And probably kittens too. I can't see heaven turning away a kitten, can you? They're all super cute, and they're still fun at that age before they become teencats and get that snooty "cattitude" Ha!)

Even if heaven opened its door or gates or whatever to all animals, Reginald probably only had a 50/50 chance of gaining entry because of his potty mouth. But I sure hope he didn't wind up "SOUTH," where it's super HOT (if you know what I mean).

Me and my friends gave Reginald a really nice funeral service. We buried him in the backyard underneath the flowerbed. I didn't just toss his stiff semi-featherless and scabby body in the dirt, in case you're wondering. Instead, I made him a nice cozy casket out of my dad's shoe box. I even added a lock of my hair for him to remember me by.

Not that dead parrots HAVE the ability to remember, but I did it anyway because you never know. (And besides, they did that a lot back in the pyramids days, like with King Tut and his coffin or sarcophagus or whatever, where they put a bunch of the dead person's junk inside the coffin with them — extra clothes and jewels, pots and pans, and knickknacks and stuff.)

I'm hoping my nice sendoff of Reggie evens the score. You know? Just in case it really was my fault that he is "no longer with us" (which are words people say when it creeps them out to use the word "died").

As you see, Reggie's death has me ~~thinking~~ obsessing about death. (Gee. Ya think?)

Not about my own. I'm only 13. I have plenty of time to obsess about that later when I'm old. Instead, I've now become super worried about my dad. And like how if something happened to my dad, what would happen to me?

Because if something happened to my dad, I would have to live with Diane, and she would NOT like that. Nope. She would not like that AT ALL! And for sure I wouldn't like it.

I don't want to alarm you or have you worry about my safety when it comes to Diane. Diane has never been abusive towards me. (Unless a lack of love and compassion is considered abuse.) She's never spanked me or even swatted my hand, not even when I was a little kid and went to touch the hot stove. But probably because that would involve skin-to-skin contact.

Believe it or not, Diane's never even yelled at me. Well, not unless it was yell to be heard from the other room. That kind of yelling she's done at least a million times.

"WILL-A! You forgot to take out the trash!"

"WILL-A! You forgot to empty the dishwasher!"

"WILL-A! You forgot to unload the dryer!"

"WILL-A! You forgot to clean the cinders from the fireplace and iron our ball gowns, and now Drizella and Anastasia and I are going to be late for the Prince's ball!"

Diane is a lot like the evil stepmothers in fairytales, except Diane has a much cuter figure.

With Olivia, she's all smoochy poo and sunshiny. With me, she's cold and distant. She never hugged me or came to my room to kiss me goodnight. She said that was my dad's job — that basically, she had "dibs" on Olivia, and Dad got stuck with me when it came to the love and affection parts of parenting.

Well, that's enough of THAT. I'm turning into a regular Miss Mary Sunshine! (Not!)

I'm gonna need to go make myself a banana split to cheer up. Fingers crossed, we have bananas! (And ice cream!)

XOXOXO,

Willa

Confessions of a Nerdy Girl: Diary #5

JUST ANOTHER MONDAY, 6:59 P.M.

Dear M,

Is there ever a good part of being a kid? Because so far, it doesn't seem like it. At least not for me. (Sorry to be such a downer all the time, but you're such a good listener. Ha!)

People expect us to be super mature when we're still just kids.

Not Kiddy — kids. It's not as if at 13 I want to sit around in my Underoos and play with paper dolls or something. But I'm also not ready to do the whole "ADULTING thing" and "PROCESS" my feelings about the divorce and the breakup of my "Nuclear Family," as my therapist suggests, either.

(And FYI — My paper doll example was for your AVERAGE girl. Personally, I've never played with paper dolls. Not at age 3. Or 4. Or 5.) Or EVER! And the only time I've sat around in my Fruit of the Loom Underoos was ... Well, more recent than I'd like to admit, and even then, it was only because I found my Superman set in the back of the closet and wanted to see if they still fit. Which they do not. Bummer.)

Super Bummer!

At what age did YOU start to feel like a "grown-up"?

Does it happen a little at a time, where every year you see a marked improvement, sort of like breast development? (Unless, of course, you're ME, and then there's no noticeable difference from one year to the next, as far as

I can tell.) Or does it come in one big AH HA! moment, when one day your brain just tells you that it's done being fully developed, which, according to science, doesn't happen until the age of 25 or so?

My dad, who is probably around your age — give or take a few years — says even most adults don't FEEL like adults. Dad says he still "emotionally" feels the same as he did at age 18. But then he also says that some days he feels 80.

Not to come off as a "nitpicker" (which means one who looks for unimportant errors or faults in order to criticize unnecessarily), but there are some things that are not GUESSABLE. My dad might feel achy and decrepit, the way he THINKS an old person must feel because he sees them bent over like a wilted celery stalk while shuffling along an inch a minute in their tattered bedroom slippers, but it would really just be conjecture on his part.

Most of my classmates can't wait to turn 16 so they can drive a car. Not me. Driving seems scary. So many split-second decisions to be made that can literally mean life or death for the driver and everyone and everything within the car's reach.

Split-second decision-making is not my strong suit. There are some mornings it takes me 20 minutes to decide which pair of jeans to wear, and they're all identical. (But they were purchased at different times, so each has a slightly different color shade, and they all feel different depending on how many times they've been washed.)

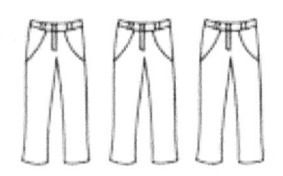

I'm cutting it short today. My therapist has given me "homework." Ugh!! As if I don't have enough going on in my life already. (And the "drawing a picture of my family" is a joke because I no longer HAVE a family.)

Willa

TRUTH OR DARE, 5:15 P.M.

Dear M,

Have you ever had a major crush on a boy? And I mean MAJOR. Like how you can't eat or sleep, and your stomach does that crazy rumble thing, and your heart beats super-fast like the rat-a-tat-tat of a firecracker snap cap every time you think about him, and how your palms get sweaty and itchy, and your underarms drip like nobody's business, and you're sort of pale but you're flushed at the same time, and you're so dizzy that whenever you stand next to him it feels as though you might faint?

That's the kind I'm talking about.

Although, MEDICAL ALERT!!

According to Marley's mom, who's a doctor and should know these things, the symptoms

Confessions of a Nerdy Girl: Diary #5

for MAJOR CRUSHES are the same symptoms that present for MALARIA, so it's best to seek medical attention if besides crushing on a guy you've also recently visited Africa, South Asia, or Papua New Guinea, to rule things out.

In case I haven't mentioned it once or twice, or a million times before, Cody Cassidy is my crush. (Well, mine, and EVERYONE else's!)

♥ ♥ ♥ ♥

One of the reasons I like Cody so much is because he's super nice to me, and he "has my back," as the saying goes. And when I tell you what happened the other day at school, you'll see what I mean.

Do you know the game Truth or Dare? It's a game where you sit in a circle, or in our case, at the lunch table, and the players take turns asking one another the question, "Truth or Dare?" If the responding person picks Truth, they have to TRUTHFULLY answer a question of the asker's choosing. If they pick Dare, the asker dares the person to do something rather than make a confession that will haunt them the rest of their lives and even after, when they're 10 feet under and worm food.

And FYI, just in case you think moving to a DESERTED island gets a middle-schooler away from the ridicule of their classmates, you'd be WRONG, because I can guarantee you that even if we moved to the farthest reaches of the earth, a message in a bottle would wash ashore with a poorly spelled essay on what a dork we are, or a skywriting airplane would do a fly-by. Not to save us but to spell out L-O-S-E-R in giant white puffs of smoke.

L•O•O•S•E•R...

Oh! Someone's at the front door. I'll be back in a jiff...

TRUTH OR DARE, CONT., 5:21 P.M.

It was an Amazon delivery. But darn. Nothing for me. My dad ordered office supplies or something.

Now, back to how to play the game.

When playing Truth or Dare, you can either move around the table in seated order, or you can spin a bottle to decide who goes first. If using the bottle method, when it stops, the bottle points to the "victim." That person has to answer the question or do the Dare. For our game, we had to go in seated order. We're not allowed glass bottles at school, and as we discovered, a wax-coated juice box just won't spin no matter how hard you try.

spins...   does not spin...

Jax went first. Technically, he wasn't sitting AT the table; he was ON TOP of it. He picked

Dare because, well, Jax's whole life is basically one big Dare anyway. Dakota told him he got his choice to either wrap his head with toilet paper like a mummy or lick his armpit. And because Jax couldn't decide which one he preferred (he loves attention!), he went to the boy's bathroom and wrapped his head in toilet paper first, and then he came back to the lunch table and tried to lick his armpit. Which, as you can imagine, was hard because his mouth was covered with toilet paper. But because it was public school toilet paper and not something nice and absorbent like Charmin, it was doable. By working up some extra spit, Jax managed to worm his tongue through the crummy paper, and so he got in a few good underarm licks before it was Dakota's turn.

Dakota chose Truth (no surprise there), and Dallas, her sister, got to ask the question.

"How many selfies do you take in a week?" Which, to a normal person, might be embarrassing, but instead turned into this lame Show and Tell with Dakota showing us a million pictures of her doing that stupid duck-lips kiss thing that people think is cute but is super dumb and makes the lips look like a baboon's ugly butt.

Cody said there should be a do-over because Dakota shows everyone her new selfies anyway without prompting. Then Braeden said Dakota should do a Truth and answer if she's ever farted in class and blamed someone else. Dakota gave Braeden a dirty look, and she whipped her head to the side in a dramatic ponytail toss, her hair landing expertly over her right shoulder, where it trailed to the middle of her stomach. (How she does that pony toss, I'll never know.)

Dakota started to pet and stroke her ponytail like she was petting a poodle, and she said with her nose up in the air, all hoity-toity, "News Flash! LADIES. DON'T. FART." And she said it in a huffy way like she was the Queen of England.

"Oh, puh-leeze!" I blurted. "That is SO not true. EVERYBODY farts, Dakota. In fact, the average person produces 500 to 1,500 milliliters of gas per day and farts between 10 and 20 times."

And here's a tip on what NOT TO SAY to a bunch of middle school kids during lunch (or EVER, really):

ANY words that make it look like you've studied fartology.

I'm not kidding, M. Even though it was lunchtime and there were hundreds of kids around, you could have heard a pin drop when everyone turned to look at me — Willa Shisbey — Triton Middle School's newest fartologist and tooty expert.

"WHAT A DORK!" Dakota said. She stopped her petting of herself and whipped her head again so that her hair landed on the back side of her, where it streamed almost to her waist like a yellow silk scarf. "What kind of gross person knows THAT kind of stuff? No wonder you don't have any friends and your moms keep running away from you. You're disgusting!"

Tears of embarrassment filled my eyes, and I looked down. "I read an article on the internet," I mumbled.

"Dakota, quit being so mean," Cody told her. "And you do too fart. You fart plenty. Remember the time..."

Dakota cut him off. "Never mind, Cody." She waved her hand like she was shooing a fly. "It's Willa's turn to go." She turned to face me. "Truth or Dare?" She said, with an evil gleam in her eyes.

Here's the deal, M. When you're me, an uncool, lame-o, nerd nugget (Olivia's words), either choice is a bad choice. Truth reveals just what a loser I really am, and Dare reveals ...

Well, I guess Dare reveals just what a loser I am, too.

Here's an example of why Truth is hazardous...

Truth: Do you drool in your sleep? (Yes.)

Truth: What's the grossest thing you've ever collected? (My toenail clippings. But (A) I was a little kid at the time, (B) It was VERY short-lived, and (C) Olivia made me throw them away or said she'd make me eat them if I didn't ditch them.)

Truth: Have you ever practiced kissing in the mirror? (Does ON the mirror count?)

Truth: Do you currently have a crush on anyone? (Duh!)

Ü ♡✱

Truth: If I went through your room, what is something I would be shocked to find? (That everything is in OCD perfect order, in a slightly scary, not-normal way.)

Truth: What was your most embarrassing moment in public? (You mean beside now? How much time do you have? A week? A year? A lifetime?)

And you just have to use your imagination to come up with hideous ideas for a Dare, but here are a few more common ones:

Pick your nose.

Dance on one leg.

Lick the ground.

Color your front tooth black with a permanent marker. (My dentist dad would freak out at that one!)

Kiss the janitor. (Who, BTW, eats sardine sandwiches for lunch. Ewww!)

So as you can imagine, I froze when Dakota asked me, Truth or Dare?

That's like asking if you want to be covered in honey and fire ants — or honey and scorpions. One is only SLIGHTLY less deadly than the other.

"Uhh ... Truth?" I replied, unconvincingly, while Dakota's face got the "cat that caught the canary" look that you hear about, which I think is a facial expression that my dad refers to as "smug."

"Tell us, Willa," she said. "What's SO wrong with you that both your birth mom AND your adoptive mom couldn't stand to be around you? Just HOW creepy are you anyway?"

I don't know if it was me who gasped or someone else, but the sound was like a loud WHOOSH, and it felt as though I had been punched in the stomach.

"NO WAY, Dakota!" Cody yelled at her. And then he looked at me as I struggled not to cry. "Willa, don't answer her," he told me. He looked away from me and wadded up his dirty napkin, and then he threw it at Dakota from across the table. Cody swung his leg over the bench, and he got up, and BOY, he was SUPER mad! I don't know that I'd ever seen Cody so mad before, his face was red, and his hands jammed down hard inside his pockets where I could see they were balled into fists.

I stared at Cody as I tried to figure out what to do. Should I try to answer Dakota's question? And what would I even say?

I DON'T KNOW why you left me, M. There could be a dozen reasons.

I was too ugly, maybe. Or I cried too much. Or you were too young to care for a baby, or maybe you had other kids, and I was a spare that you didn't need or couldn't afford to keep. Believe me; there isn't a day that goes by that I don't wonder why you gave me away.

And I also don't know why Diane hated me so much that she'd rather split our family apart than to live in a house with me. I'm not noisy. I'm not disrespectful. (Out loud, anyway. Inside my mind, I can be bratty sometimes.) I keep my bedroom and bathroom and my body ridiculously clean. I'm appreciative of the nice life that I have and the love of my dad and my friends.

"DARE, Willa," Cody said to me, bringing me back to the present, his voice loud enough for the group to hear. And then Cody dropped his voice so that only I could hear him. "Trust me. You need to trust me." And I nodded that I did trust him. I'd trust Cody with my life.

"Willa," he said, loud enough for everyone around us to hear. "I Dare you to go up on the quad and sing 'Yankee Doodle Dandy.'"

I felt my heart drop to my toes and the tiniest bit of vomit sting the back of my throat.

Our quad is sort of this raised area with concrete and grass, and it has our flagpole in the middle of it. It also has a microphone where the principal makes announcements. Cody was basically asking me to go up on a big stage and sing in front of half of the school! Although how he figured out I actually knew the words to that song was anyone's guess.

Cody jogged across the lunch area, and after negotiating with the lunch aide to use the mic, he tapped it to make sure it was working, and he said, "Ladies and gentlemen, I give you Willa Shisbey! Come on up, Willa."

With legs that felt like overcooked spaghetti, I wobbled on up, trying not to puke.

"You sing, Willa, and the guys and I will do the rest," he softly said, pointing to his friends at the table and waving them over to join us. "And I've heard you hum the song before, so I KNOW that you know it."

And that's how I wound up singing (off-key) while Cody and his fellow scout-mates did an elaborate and slightly comical, pseudo-military-slash-show-tunes dance worthy of a Scout-O-Rama closing ceremony, while I warbled onstage like a seasick pelican:

"I'm a Yankee Doodle Dandy, A Yankee Doodle, do or die; A real live nephew of my Uncle Sam's, Born on the Fourth of July. I've got a Yankee Doodle sweetheart. She's my Yankee Doodle joy. Yankee Doodle came to

London just to ride the ponies; I am the Yankee Doodle Boy!"

That's just the chorus. Despite what Cody said, it's the only part of the song that I (and most everyone else on the planet) actually know.

The chorus wasn't quite long enough to let the boys finish their dance routine, so I had to sing it twice through. Plus, there was a major mess up when Dylan began marching in the wrong direction and bumped into Jax, who tripped Cody, who fell and forced Braeden into the flagpole, where it smashed his nose, which started to bleed. It wasn't bleeding buckets or anything like that, and it sort of added to the whole red, white, and blue Americana thing anyway, which everyone loved.

They ended their performance with all of the boys in a straight line saluting the flag. And I KID YOU NOT; by the time I was on the second round of the song, half of the lunch kids were singing along, which says a lot about the power of "The Theater" because the song was written in 1904 for a Broadway musical, in case you didn't know.

After my song ended, Dakota was so mad that her evil plan failed that she and Dallas, and the rest of her minions left the area (although by then, the bell rang, so maybe they just needed to get to class.)

And I have to say that it might have been one of the more embarrassing moments of my life, but it was sort of fun too.

That's all for now.

Love,

Willa

ANOTHER UGLY PUGLY DAY, 7:47 P.M.

Dear M,

Was it super important to be cute back when you were in middle school? Because it sure is important these days.

My dad says that "beauty is only skin deep," which means that it's more important what's inside, like our character and morals and stuff, than the reflection we see looking back at us in the mirror.

And not to disrespect my dad, but I say — Baloney, Salami!

If you've EVER seen the social media post of a teen, you'd know that every second of every day, one needs to be Perfectly Picture Perfect. And if you can't make that happen naturally, then you need to fake it using dumb face apps where everyone looks like little Betty Lou Who from Whoville, with big rounded eyes, super long eyelashes, and oversized blinding white teeth that look like they came out of a Chiclets gum pack.

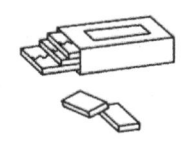

Because it DOES matter what we look like on the outside! It REALLY matters. One can be WITTY, and KIND, and...

uh ... and ...

uhh ...

(I was referencing myself with my use of the word "One," in case you couldn't tell, but I've seemed to have run out of my good qualities.)

Anyway, my point is — that unless we're cute, life is NOT opening the front door and welcoming us inside, if you get my drift.

People that look like me don't get picked to be on the Dodge Ball team; they get to be the TARGET. (Have you ever had a Dodge Ball slam to the face? It'll make you cry! Seriously, I can't believe Dodge Ball hasn't been outlawed by now. Someone needs to do an undercover story regarding all the unreported Dodge Ball deaths and maimings.)

People like me don't get chosen as prom queen. Instead, we get assigned to the Clean-Up Crew because, let's face it, everyone knows we won't be doing anything after the dance anyway.

100 times out of 100, pretty wins.

100 ♥:

What we see when we look in the mirror matters. It matters BIG TIME!

BIG TIME! BIG TIME! BIG TIME!

Believe me; there's a huge difference between what Dakota and Dallas Duncan see when they look in the mirror and the mug that I see looking back at me.

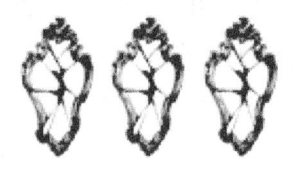

People like Dakota and Dallas, and Olivia see a gorgeous face with perfectly arched brows, clear skin, and lips that seem perpetually glossed.

My mirror shows a head too big for my body, thick bushy eyebrows a few hairs short of a unibrow, zits galore (both pre and post-eruption), and lips perpetually chapped no matter how much Burt's Bees I glob on them. (FYI: Burt's Bees is a brand of lip balm. It's not made from actual bees as far as I know, but it probably has honey or something in it as their "gimmick.")

Add a pair of oversized glasses, drab hair, a scar above my lip where my cleft used to be, and I'm a WONDER to behold for sure!

My BFF Marley promises that someday I'll "grow into" what Marley calls my "Girl Next Door" natural good looks. I'm not sure what that means, but if it's coming from Marley, it has to be something nice.

In the meantime, I'll try to minimize the horror that is puberty by slathering on the acne cream and investing in a new pair of tweezers since Olivia stole my only pair. I don't want to go all TMI on you, but my eyebrows are now so hairy that I've named them Thing 1 and Thing 2.

Yours in hairiness,

Willa

Confessions of a Nerdy Girl: Diary #5

A RAINY FRIDAY, 8:02 P.M.

Dear M,

Have you ever done a "Family Tree" before?

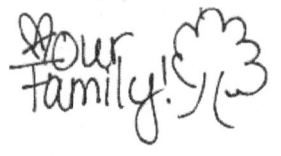

Our Family!

It's one of those dumb things you do in second or third grade, where you draw a picture of a tree that has branches extending out to the right and then an equal amount to the left, and then you fill in the leaves with the names of all of your family members going back to the beginning of time when everyone frolicked around in fur bikinis and invented wheels and discovered fire and stuff.

HA! Just kidding.

Confessions of a Nerdy Girl: Diary #5

The family tree was supposed to be the "written part" of the Baby Think It Over project that I mentioned before. Miss Meek said she felt it was a good way to "get to know a little more about your classmates." My answer to her (but in my MIND, cuz I didn't have the guts to say it aloud) was that I knew my classmates PLENTY!

I knew them to be mean-spirited, snobby, and so cliquey that a newcomer like me never had a chance of being accepted to the group.

We only had to go as far back as our great grandparents, but for me — one generation or one hundred — it doesn't matter because I still come up with NADA - ZIP - ZERO in the leaf department.

What kind of loser has NO leaves on their tree because they have no real family? (Not that YOU'RE not real, M, but I don't think you count because even though I know you once existed, I don't have certifiable proof that you still do, and for now, you're just an idea in my head.)

My dad told me to use his side of the family for the assignment, but they're all deceased (poor dad), and it was too depressing to keep writing:

Deceased

Deceased

Deceased

Diane's side is still alive and kicking, but Diane said she "wasn't comfortable" revealing her family's personal information to me (as if they're all in the Witness Protection Program or something and having their names on a middle school assignment might be life threatening in some way. (*Insert eye roll here.)

And not only did we need to fill out the family tree as part of the project, but then we were supposed to have an oral presentation in front of the class! (*Insert gonna vomit face here.)

I wanted to tell Miss Meek — IN PRIVATE, that I'm adopted, and that's why I had a problem with filling out the tree. But then dumb Dakota had to open her big yap and announce to the ENTIRE CLASS that I was a "changeling," and you left me in a basket on the front steps of an orphanage, and that's why I couldn't fill out the tree.

But as we both know, (1) you did not leave me in a BASKET on the front steps of the orphanage. Instead, you gently handed me off to the lady who opened the door, and (2) even if you did leave me in a basket on the front steps, that would make me a FOUNDLING — which is an infant that has been abandoned by its parents and is discovered and cared for by others — NOT a CHANGELING, which in fairytales is an ugly, stupid, or strange child left by fairies in place of a pretty, charming child. (Although, now I see that Dakota actually had a strong case.)

So instead of doing a lame family tree like the rest of the class, do you know what I did? With Miss Meek's permission, I drew a flower garden instead. I titled my picture and essay "People Who Make Me Bloom," with each flower representing a person who's made a difference in my life.

When I got up to read it, I was soooo nervous I thought for sure I was gonna hurl. But as my dad says, I just "powered through," and this is what I said:

Confessions of a Nerdy Girl: Diary #5

"I don't know who my birth mother is — or my birth father. And now my adoptive parents are getting divorced, so it will just be my dad and me. That's why I couldn't fill out the family tree on my project. Because I don't really have what most people consider family. So instead, I did a garden."

I held up the colored picture I'd drawn, but I covered Cody's name written on the aster, a flower I chose because asters symbolize love, good luck, and victorious battles. Marley's name was in cursive, and it looped around her flower, the Black-Eyed Susan. (Which, looking back, makes it seem like I'm insensitive of her heritage, but which I chose because Black-Eyed Susans are known to be a competitive flower and a prolific bloomer, which is Marley to a "T.")

Sam's name trailed up the goldenrod on the bottom of the page, a flower that blooms hardy and tall and stands freely without support, much like Sam, who, despite losing her mom to cancer and living in a car, still attended school and rocked at being the co-parent of our fake baby.

"I titled my garden, 'People Who Make Me Bloom,'" I said, my voice as wobbly as my knees while standing with my back to the blackboard (although our board is green, not black) and facing the class.

I stuttered my way through a bunch of "Uhhs..." and "Umms," but eventually, I got the words to dribble out of my mouth.

"Each flower in my garden represents a person — someone who's made a difference in my life. The flowers I chose are called perennials because, unlike annual flowers that only bloom for a single season and then need replacing, perennials bloom for many years."

By then, my hands were shaking so hard that the papers slipped out of my fingers and scattered on the floor. Some of the kids started to laugh but were shushed by Miss Meek. I bent to the floor and then stood and reassembled the papers.

When I got the pages back in order, I continued. "I also learned that Miss Meek was right when she told us last Tuesday — and I'll quote her now — 'In my opinion, family no longer refers to only a mom and a dad and a child. To me, a family is an environment where two or more bond together to love and nurture.'"

Dakota said, "OH BROTHER!" really loud, and she made a gagging sound, but Miss Meek gave her the stink eye, so she quit.

I looked over the heads of the first few rows to search out Cody, who, besides Marley, is my closest friend. (And who I not-so-secretly L.O.V.E. But then, who DOESN'T love Cody Cassidy?) Cody watched me, his body perfectly still as if he was holding his breath, nervous for me, knowing that I'm not good with talking in front of people.

I held his gaze for just a moment before saying, "Let me tell you what I think makes a family."

My heart hammered so loudly I thought for SURE the class could hear it. Cody nodded at me, a crooked smile on his adorable face, and he gave me two thumbs up, encouraging me to continue.

"LOVE — makes you family ... And, TRUST."

Cody blushed, but not half as much as I did because, basically, I just told Cody and the WHOLE class that I love him! (Eeks!)

Then I stood on my tiptoes to find Sam's face at the back of the room — Sam, my friend and co-parent of my fake baby, where she sat at our shared desk looking at me like she was gonna barf too because she felt my pain and knew that at any moment I might faint from fear.

"SACRIFICE — is family," I said, speaking directly to Sam, and my voice caught on the words so it sounded like I was going to cry. "And LOYALTY — beyond measure," I added.

"Thank you," I mouthed to Sam, emotionally blocking out all the people in the room so that it was just the two of us for a second. Sam put her palms together, gave a slight dip of her head, and she mouthed, "You're welcome."

Marley isn't in my class (she has all AP classes), so I couldn't speak directly to her.

I scanned the faces of my classmates— Keiran, Jax, Dallas, Brylee, Dylan, and the rest, kids just like me, each with his or her own problems and each with families who were less than perfect. If I'd learned little over those couple of weeks, I learned this: It doesn't matter who gave us life, but rather, who SUSTAINS it.

It shouldn't matter that Miss Meek's definition of "family" is herself and the three cats she adores or that my version of family is a party of two: a divorced dad and his adopted daughter. Or for Sam, that it's a widower with two kids who, rather than be split apart by poverty, were able to make a van their home. Family is as diverse as the flowers in my dad's garden.

And sometimes, a "family" might have no parents at all because I was a kid who grew up in an orphanage, and the boys and girls became my family — and the staff too.

In the end, when you really think about it, M, just having someone to love is FAMILY.

Cody started clapping when I finished, and because everyone has to do what Cody does (it's an unwritten rule or something), everyone joined in. Even Dakota, if you can believe that. (Although her clap was sort of sarcastic, and she basically just tapped two fingers of her right hand into the bottom palm of her left.)

And that's it. That's how I defined family.

But between you and me, in my heart of hearts (and this happens especially when I'm sad, which seems to happen a lot lately), someday, somehow, I still hope to find you. Not because I don't love my dad, because I do. I love him tons. But because I still have so many unanswered questions, and I feel sort of lost, like I need to find the road again. I think that the only real way to know where I'm going is to know where I've been ...

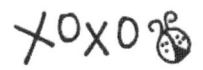

XOXO

Love,

Willa

GRATITUDE SUNDAY, 10:10 A.M.

Dear M,

Writing this diary has helped me to put some things in perspective.

I don't know if you'll ever get a chance to read it, or even if you should. It might make things harder for us, you know? Like maybe I've hurt your feelings with the things I've said or that I've asked questions that don't have easy answers.

People change as they get older. I know I have. And choices that seem right at the time sometimes don't seem nearly so rock-solid later on. (Example: Getting bangs in the 4th grade. Seriously? Does ANYONE look good in bangs? Taylor Swift — maybe. But she'd be the first.)

I know in my heart of hearts that you thought long and hard before you left me at the orphanage and that it wasn't an easy decision. I know that you did it out of your love for me and with the hope that I'd get a shot at a better life — despite what Olivia says, that you ditched me because you couldn't stand to see my messed-up face.

It's been good for me to share my feelings with you in the pages of these diaries. Even my therapist thinks so. She says that everyone should journal and that it can help us gain control of our emotions and provide an opportunity for positive self-talk. (I'm still working on that one!) She also says journaling shouldn't just be for confused teenagers but for everyone who wants to understand their thoughts and feelings more clearly. She says journaling helps to manage anxiety, reduce stress, and cope with depression. (Check. Check. And double check.) If YOU haven't tried it, I highly recommend it!

Do you want to know what I've learned over the past few months? And not just from writing in the pages of this diary, but from doing a "deep-dive," as my therapist calls it, into my "psyche" (which is just a fancy way of saying "my mind.")

I've learned that no matter how things may look on the outside, we don't know what's happening on the inside. Like, how great Dakota's and Dallas's life seem to the world, all beauty and glamour and wealth, but how behind the doors of the castle lies chambers of secrets and mean hairy trolls. (Not literally — the hairy troll part. But I know there are plenty of secrets.)

Or how Cody's family, another rich, seemingly perfect McLovin' family with a lifetime of free cheeseburgers, has discord and prejudice and other major parent-child issues that could easily be solved with a little non-judgement and understanding.

And then, in reverse, where things may seem bad or challenging on the outside, there's Marley, who deals with racial prejudice all of the time and yet who has a home filled with warmth and intelligence and laughter galore.

Or Sam, who learned that the definition of HOME isn't four walls but, rather, a warm space for friends and family to come together in purpose and love — even if that space is a ratty old van.

And Robbie, my friend with cerebral palsy, who, let's face it, could be mad at the world if he wanted (because, according to him, the worst thing about CP is that he can't scratch his own nose!) And yet who inspires us all with his optimism and humor, saying, "When it comes right down to it, Willa, the most important muscle isn't the one in my leg or my arms, it's my BRAIN, and it's as big and fit and strong as they come." To which I say, Rock On!

Rock On ♥

I've also thought a lot about the Truth or Dare game and how it's sort of like life. That there are times we need to pick Truth and examine our feelings or talk to someone who can help us to sort out our chaotic emotions and put our life in perspective. But then there are other times when we need to challenge ourselves and pick Dare, when we stare fear in the face and hock a big one at it. (Sorry, sounds gross, I know.) Or maybe we don't hock. Maybe we just work up a little spit so it's a gentle pffftttt.

I've learned that the breakup of a family is hard. The death of a pet is hard. Rejection is hard. Let's face it; LIFE is hard! And there are times when the days are dark despite the bright California sun. But I'm working on seeing my glass as half-full instead of nearly empty. I'm working on loving myself, the person staring back at me in the mirror, despite the glasses, the zits, and the scar on my face.

I know I'm not like other kids. I'll always have crystal clear memories of my time in an orphanage, of being an outsider, of being the reason for my dad's divorce (despite his insistence that it wasn't my fault.) But I now realize there is WAY more to be happy about than there is to be sad about.

There is friendship. There is health. There is hope.

And maybe tomorrow, or next week, or next year, I'll have a new list of what I'm happy for, but for now, I'll hang on to the possibility that there are better things coming my way ... That maybe someday I'll grow into a B cup. Or I'll get LASIK and not need glasses. Or that I'll even reconnect with you.

And I couldn't ask for more than that.

With much love,

Your daughter,

Willa

Nerdy Girl books by Linda Rey

Diary Series:

TOP SECRET: Diary #1 (Confessions of a Nerdy Girl Diaries)

UNLUCKY THIRTEEN: Diary #2 (Confessions of a Nerdy Girl Diaries)

LETTERS FROM SUMMER CAMP: Diary #3 (Confessions of a Nerdy Girl Diaries)

LETTERS TO SANTA, THE EASTER BUNNY, AND OTHER LAME STUFF: Diary #4 (Confessions of a Nerdy Girl Diaries)

TRUTH OR DARE: Diary #5 (Confessions of a Nerdy Girl Diaries)

SUNNY SIDE OVER: Diary #6 (Confessions of a Nerdy Girl Diaries) Coming Soon!

Novel Series:

NERDY EVER AFTER: A Nerdy Novel, Book 1 (Confessions of a Nerdy Girl)

CHECK OUT ALL OF THE NEWEST TITLES AND OTHER NERDY NEWS AT:

www.nerdygirlbooks.com

ABOUT THE AUTHOR

Linda Rey was born with the voice of an angel and a brain so amazing she'll probably donate it to science. When she's not busy *fa la la-ing* from the hilltops or doing fantastical brain stuff in laboratories, Linda can be found at her computer creating lives far more interesting than her own.

To see all of Linda's titles for younger readers visit her website at www.LindaReyBooks.com and www.NerdyGirlBooks.com or you can email her at – linda@lindareybooks.com (And yes, that's her real email, unless you don't have something nice to say – then no, it's not.)

Made in the USA
Monee, IL
22 January 2025